ONE PEOPLE
MANY TRIBES
A primer on Church History from a Messianic Jewish perspective.

KAIROS PUBLISHING

DANIEL C. JUSTER
& PATRICIA A. JUSTER

Note to the Reader

This book has been transcribed and edited from a series of lectures presented by Dr. Daniel C. Juster.

PUBLISHED BY KAIROS PUBLISHING
PO Box 450, Clarence, NY 14031
PHONE: 716.759.1058 FAX: 716.759.0731
EMAIL: kairos@eagleswings.to
WEBSITE: www.eagleswings.to

ISBN 0-9665831-1-6
Copyright © 1999 Daniel C. Juster
All rights reserved.
Printed in the United States of America
November 1999
First Edition
No part of this book may be used or reproduced in any manner without written permission except in the case of brief quotations for the use of personal and/or group study. This book may not be copied or reprinted for commercial gain or profit.
Scripture taken from The Holy Bible, New International Version
Copyright © 1973, 1978, 1984

Book & Cover design by Paul Saran Carroll.
Cover photo: Jen Wong/Photonica ©1999

To order additional copies call or write to :
Eagles' Wings, PO Box 450, Clarence, NY 14031
Phone: 716.759.1058 Fax: 716.759.0731
Email: orders@eagleswings.to
WEBSITE: www.eagleswings.to

ONE PEOPLE MANY TRIBES

Dan Juster is a significant voice that God has raised up in the Church today. Through the lenses of Church History, "One People Many Tribes" provides sound Biblical understanding for the purpose, focus, and direction of the Church. I especially recommend this book for anyone seeking to better understand the importance of the Church's role and relationship with Israel as it relates to the full restoration of the Church into all that God has called her.

Mike Bickle
EXECUTIVE DIRECTOR, FRIENDS OF THE BRIDEGROOM

In a day where authentic unity in the Church is so desperately needed, "One People Many Tribes" is a breath of fresh air. In this overview of Church History, Dan Juster explains how the Church's attitude toward Israel and a more Biblical understanding of her Jewish roots provide very significant keys for releasing greater measures of unity within the Body of Christ.

Larry Kreider
INTERNATIONAL DIRECTOR, D.O.V.E CHRISTIAN FELLOWSHIP INTERNATIONAL

Dan Juster is a voice - a forerunner - helping to prepare the Body of Messiah to be all we are called to be. With a deep commitment to theological integrity and the power of the Spirit, Dan is providing vital leadership in this crucial hour. This book will serve to help bridge the gap between Jew and Gentile, and aid us in moving together as "one new man" in Yeshua.

Robert Stearns
EXECUTIVE DIRECTOR, EAGLES' WINGS

Through this Messianic perspective of Church History, Dan Juster shares how a greater understanding of the Church's Jewish roots provides a more accurate awareness of her identity as a partner with God in His purposes being released in the earth. "One People Many Tribes" wonderfully puts into focus the importance of Israel and the Jewish roots of the Church for a greater self-awareness of every believer in the Body of Christ.

Don Finto
SENIOR PASTOR, BELMONT FAMILY OF CHURCHES

CONTENTS

Introduction
Understanding Church History — 1

Chapter One
New Covenant History — 7

Chapter Two
The Early Church : *The Beginnings of Decline* — 25

Chapter Three
The Beginnings of the Catholic Church — 35

Chapter Four
The Reformation — 49

Chapter Five
The Anabaptists — 63

Chapter Six
The Anglican Church — 69

Chapter Seven
The Puritan Movement — 75

Chapter Eight
The Methodist Movement — 85

Chapter Nine
The Beginnings of Christian Zionism — 91

Chapter Ten
Restoration Movements in the United States — 97

Chapter Eleven
Conclusion — 121

Summary — 129

ONEPEOPLE MANY TRIBES

*This book is dedicated to all those
who give themselves to the unity of the Church
and the restoration of Israel.*

Daniel C. Juster
September 23, 1999

INTRODUCTION
UNDERSTANDING CHURCH HISTORY

UNDERSTANDING CHURCH HISTORY

Understanding the church rightly is very important for those of us who consider ourselves to be a part of the Messianic Jewish Movement, both Jew and Gentile. We are not going to be able to fulfill our task in this movement of the restored remnant if we are not rightly related to the church. This includes not only our relatedness to individuals, but also our relatedness to an understanding of the church. I believe this is essential.

This is not just a brief summary of Church History. It is history with a perspective - a perspective which I believe the Lord has given me. Of course, there are going to be some inaccuracies in any perspective, but I trust that it is going to be helpful and basically true.

WHAT IS THE MEANING OF HISTORY?

The way we examine history is dependent on whether we view history as having meaning or purpose to its direction (Biblical view), or whether we view history as just a collection of successive events and facts which may have a certain historical causation in them (secular view). The necessary implication of the latter view, a view held by most secular historians, is that the study of history involves the examination of a collection of facts which lends itself to self interest for the process of interpretation. However, if, as in the Biblical view, you believe that God is the Lord of history and you believe that the center of history is to be found in the history of Israel and the Church, then one finds that the real reasons behind historical events are found in the principle of sowing and reaping. History takes on a whole different interpretation; it teaches us lessons about the ways of God.[1]

The best writing of history is the history of Israel and the Church found in the writings of Numbers, Kings, Chronicles, and the book of Acts. In the Bible, history is understood from the perspective of what God is seeking to do through the ages. It is the discerning of what God is doing in the earth.

My understanding of history, and I'll put this in the context of broad universal history, is that the history of other cultures and their quality of life is related to what they did with the revelation that was given from Noah, since all nations are descended from Noah. Most cultures have some memory of the Fall and some memory of the Flood.[2]

But God chose a people in the midst of the earth, called the nation of Israel, to restore and extend His truth to the nations. They were to be the keeper of this revelation and the source through which God would turn the world back to Himself. History is the story of this redemption. Biblically, once Israel has done its job of restoring God's truth in the Middle East, and then after Yeshua returns to the earth, the Kingdom of God will expand out of Israel to the nations of the world.[3]

Putting history into this broader context of sowing (God's revelation sown among the nations) and reaping (what the nations have done with this revelation) says to me that history is God's story of what the world has done with the Gospel, what the world has done with the Noahic revelation, and what the world has done with the revelation of God through nature (Romans 1).

That is the center of discernment in history.

1 I believe that the primary reason why many people view history as a boring topic is because it has often been taught mostly as a collection of mere facts. History was never meant to be taught this way.

2 Not all cultures do, but most regions of the world do. There was revelation that came down to the human race from Noah. Most nations and cultures, more or less, repudiated that revelation or allowed that revelation to be perverted.

3 Discernment is needed in interpreting history concerning the direction of the nations that have not heard the Gospel of the Kingdom in contrast with those nations that have heard the Gospel. What have the nations who have heard the Gospel done with the opportunity given them?

CHAPTER ONE
NEW COVENANT HISTORY

NEW COVENANT HISTORY

In the book of Acts we have the beginning of the history of a new thing in the midst of the earth. It was not new with regard to the fact that there was not a people of God on earth before - the people of Israel were the people of God. They were a nation of saved people; the whole nation was not saved in terms of every individual in it, but Israel was corporately the people of God. Now, in Acts, a New Covenant comes; a new revelation. I think it is important to understand the newly introduced "apostolic perspective" in launching the Body of Believers, which came to be known after many language transitions as the Church.[4]

The center of history now is in the kehillah of Yeshua. Kehillah is the word in Aramaic or Hebrew for "congregation" and Yeshua said:

> *Upon this rock* - <u>the rock of the confession of My kingship; the confession of My Messiahship because I am the King of the Kingdom of God, I am the King that rules on the Davidic throne</u> - *upon this confession I will build my kehillah (congregation), and the gates of hell will not prevail against it. (Matthew 16:18)*

The disciples did not understand the implications of what Yeshua was saying and doing at the time He said this, anymore than we today have a full understanding of the Scriptures outside years of study and the Holy Spirit opening them up to us. Yeshua was creating a peoplehood within the midst of the earth that would be a manifestation of His Kingdom.

The terminology that we use in the Body of Believers today is so skewed that even we do not see the importance of what Yeshua said. Even the phrases that we use: "Go to church," or "Where do you go to church?" are an unbiblical way of speaking which blinds us to what the Scripture is saying.

We don't "go to church." We are the Church. We go to an expression of worship of the corporate Body. We go to a meeting for teaching, to be equipped by the leadership of that corporate Body. The fact that the word "church" has its true background in the word "kehillah/congregation" shows us how skewed our terminology is. Replace the word "church," which also refers to a building, with "congregation." If you say, "Where do you go to congregation?" you will realize how false the view is that church is something you go to rather than something you are as a people.

THE DISCIPLES' UNDERSTANDING OF GOD'S PLAN

The doctrine of the keys in Matthew 16 ("I give you the keys of the kingdom.") refers to the authority to make the judicial decisions in Israel. Another passage that indicates a transference of judicial authority to the disciples is found in Matthew 18:18: "Whatever you bind on earth will be bound in heaven." This means that they would have the authority to decide what people would be loosed from and what they would be bound to do. Before this time, the authority was limited to the judicial body of Israel, the Sanhedrin.

Yeshua said, "I will establish my congregation and the gates of hell will not prevail against it." The disciples had probably figured, "Great! There's going to be a synagogue within Israel! It's going to be real strong." Their perspective after Matthew 16 was that Yeshua was transferring the authority from the Sanhedrin to themselves.

After Yeshua died on the cross and was resurrected, the disciples came to a fuller understanding of what this transference of authority was all about. At first their Messiah's death shocked them because they thought that He was going to come and fulfill the prophecies to deliver Israel from foreign oppression. They had hoped that the glorious deliverance the Messiah would bring would issue in the Age to Come[5] in fullness. Instead, Yeshua hung on a cross. Three days later He was resurrected. The disciples were gloriously encouraged!

He taught His disciples for forty days, and yet even then they still did not understand everything. Forty days passed and Yeshua was on the Mount of Olives. They did not know what was going on. Picture it! Familiarity breeds not only contempt but a lack of perception of the fullness of what is going on. It is very important that we are able to see this afresh.

They said, "Will You at this time restore the Kingdom to Israel?" In other words, "Will You at this time do what the Messiah is supposed to do - deliver us from the Romans, bring that glorious deliverance the prophets spoke of, and then we will see the Kingdom Age come in fullness?" **They didn't yet understand that Yeshua was bringing forth a stage of Kingdom manifestation that was partial and would be expressed in the healed lives of believers through their quality of love and justice within the congre-**

gations of Yeshua.

Yes, we are to create communities of love and justice in the way we treat each other, and we are to enforce the standards of God (understanding that we receive the grace for keeping those standards). The nature of what the disciples understood was very different than what Yeshua was trying to convey - *the partial but real manifestation of the Kingdom through the Body of Believers and their involvement in every realm of life.* This is what Yeshua brought. The disciples, however, were still looking for the war against Rome and the deliverance. Here they were for forty days, learning why Yeshua had to die, and learning about the prophetic Scriptures which He had fulfilled. At this point they were on the Mount of Olives overlooking Jerusalem, and their focus was, "Well it's about ready to happen now. We've been through seminary, we've got our degrees, now we're going to throw off the Romans; we're going to bring in the Kingdom Age." Thus, it is in this context they asked, "Will you at this time restore the Kingdom to Israel?"

Yeshua answered, "It's not for you to know the times or the seasons! (Acts 1:7)"

Contrary to what is taught in many sectors of the church, Yeshua did not say or imply, "Don't you understand that I'm not into that? I'm here to bring in a spiritual kingdom. I'm not here to bring this external worldwide millennial kingdom; you're theology is off; you're still thinking carnally, you've got to be spiritual." Literally, there are many sermons that imply such a reasoning of Yeshua. Such teaching is simply out of context and wrong. Because Yeshua said, "It is not for you to know the times or the seasons" many interpret His view of the Kingdom wrongly.

Rather, what Yeshua meant was, "Yes, what you're expecting is right. It **is** going to come, but **not yet**. First you must go to Jerusalem and there wait for the promise of the Father. You are going to receive power after the Holy Spirit comes on you and then you are going to become witnesses - first in Jerusalem, Judea, and in Samaria, and then to the uttermost parts of the earth" (Acts 1:8).

Then Yeshua was taken up into the heavens and the disciples were amazed. An angel appeared and said, "Why stand you gazing up into heaven? This same Yeshua whom you have seen will come again in like manner as you have seen Him go" (Acts 1:11).

The disciples had no idea that Yeshua's return would take 2,000 plus years! So the last instruction they had was to go to Jerusalem and wait. They went and waited, and there a wonderful miracle took place. The Spirit was poured out on 120 faithful disciples. They spoke in other languages. There was a great rush of wind, and tongues of fire seemed to rest upon them all. They went out onto the street and preached the Good News to the Jewish people that had gathered from all over the world for the Feast of Shauvot (the Feast of Pentecost). Thousands responded. Remember that these people from all the nations that were now gathered in Jerusalem were Jews that spoke different languages because they resided in different countries.

THE DISCIPLES' UNDERSTANDING GROWS

The disciples had an eschatology (an understanding of how history would develop at the end of the age). Their thinking was probably something like this: "Well, of course! Before He overthrows the Romans, we've got to get Israel to repent! Now, we understand!" Well, they did understand... partially. They believed that once Israel accepted Yeshua as the Messiah-King, then the Romans would be overthrown, and then the Kingdom would come in fullness.

Did you ever ask yourself why there was no mission to the Gentiles through the first ten chapters of the book of Acts? Yeshua taught, "You will receive power after the Holy Spirit comes upon you, and you will be My witnesses in Judea, Samaria and to the uttermost parts of the earth." They probably thought, "Ah! We've got to share this with the Jewish people all over the world, wherever Jews reside!" They weren't thinking of Jerusalem, Judea, and Samaria as places to share this with the **Gentiles**; they were only thinking about the **Jews**! They did, however, share the Gospel with the Samaritans, but only after a scattering from persecution (Acts 8).

Look at Mathew 28:19. Yeshua said, "Therefore go and make disciples of all nations..." Obviously the disciples did not understand Jesus' words. Perhaps their thinking was, "Of course! We'll disciple all the nations when Yeshua returns. After Israel has repented and been delivered, then we'll go out and disciple all the nations." I believe this is how they thought. They put Yeshua's words in the framework of a first century Jewish understanding of the nature of how history would develop. They were looking forward to Israel repenting, after which they were expecting the Messiah to come. In Acts 3:21, Peter said to an all Jewish audience, "Repent that God might send Yeshua, who must remain in heaven until the times of the restoration of all things (Age to Come) spoken by the mouth of all His holy prophets since the world began." He must remain in heaven "until" the times of the restoration. That "until" is connected to Israel repenting and receiving Him corporately as the Messianic King.[6]

Within the framework of first century Judaism the disciples probably reasoned like this: "Mission to the Gentiles? Why would we want to do that? All we have to do is get Israel saved and then, of course, the nations will all come! The blinders over the minds of the nations will be removed when Israel fully embraces Yeshua" (Isaiah 25 spoke of the blindness over the nations being removed)."

GOD'S PLAN FOR THIS AGE

The disciples were in for a big surprise on two fronts. First, they had no idea that they had a mission at this time to the Gentiles. Second, they had no idea that Israel would say "No" to their preaching of the Good News. They had the testimony of the Resurrection. They had the empty tomb. They had signs and wonders like the world had never seen. They probably figured it would be only a matter of time - even a brief period of time - until all Israel would believe.

I believe that part of the reason the disciples were unable to understand what Yeshua was saying was because they did not fully understand Daniel 9. My understanding of Daniel 9 is a little different from Dispensationalist thought. I believe that the one who confirmed the covenant in verse 27 is the Messiah who confirmed the covenant in His ministry for $3^{1/2}$ years. Then the disciples confirmed it in Jerusalem for three and a half years. This is seven years. You can see that in the midst of the 70th week, Yeshua died and caused sacrifice and oblation to cease, at least in terms of its centrality because of His own sacrifice. The covenant was confirmed for the last half of the 70th week in the apostolic preaching. Then the judgment fell. You can find the verification of this in the Talmud. It says that the cord outside of the Temple after Yom Kippur (The Day of Atonement) no longer turned from red to white as an indication of the acceptance of the sacrifices. This happened during the days of the disciples in Jerusalem, forty years before the destruction of the Temple.

The doors of the Temple swung open during the days of Johannan ben Zakkai, signifying judgment was coming. The Talmud dates the decree of judgement to forty years earlier, which is the same time the Talmud dated that the cord outside the Temple ceased to turn from red to white. This would have been the time of the confirmation of the covenant. Then the prince (Titus) would come and destroy the city and the sanctuary according to verse 26. God had allowed one forty year generation of mercy before the actual judgment fell.

The disciples probably believed that Israel would accept their witness. However, that Israel would reject their witness and that the Temple would be destroyed was predicted in Daniel 9. Their view was that Israel would accept Yeshua, then be delivered from Roman domination, and then Jesus would return leading to the salvation of the nations. This does not fit Daniel 9 which indicates that Israel rejects the covenant after a seven year offer. Though unforeseen, the Gentile mission will be a key to Israel's salvation.

The disciples found that most of the religious leaders weren't about to accept the miracle. If they had accepted the resurrection of Yeshua, what would have happened? They would have had to step down and submit to the apostles' authority! Thus, Israel was led astray by their leaders. Only a remnant, a large minority in this case, believed. The remnant that believed, that was growing, now had to be given a part of the puzzle they never dreamed of. They never dreamed that there was to be a community of Jew and Gentile together in this age, before Israel was delivered, that would be the Bride of the Messiah. This would be the key to Israel's believing and being re-ingrafted, even the key to the fulfillment of Israel being delivered from her oppressors!

Do you see historically that God is setting up the same circumstances today as in the first century? It is all going to happen again! Only this time the deliverance that the Apostles expected will come, but the key to that deliverance is going to be the prayer and witness of the whole Body of Believers - the Jewish remnant members of that Body, as well as the Gentiles. In Romans 11:11 Paul makes an astounding statement. He said, "Salvation has come to the Gentiles **for the purpose** of making Israel jealous!" In other words, Paul was a Jew and said, "I magnify my ministry, if by any means I may provoke to jealousy those who are of my flesh and save some of them." Paul is a representative of the saved remnant of Israel. He is speaking to the body of Gentile believers and saying that they are to follow his example in making Israel jealous, so they together - both Jewish and Gentile believers - will make Israel jealous. Then, Israel will be grafted back in, and when the nation turns to Yeshua, the mighty deliverance will come so that the words of Peter will be fulfilled, "Repent, that God might send Yeshua!" **The return of Yeshua is still contingent, I believe, on Jewish repentance.**

Paul also says that the key to bringing Israel to faith in Yeshua is the Body of Believers (the Church). This was a mystery that was not previously seen clearly by the prophets (Ephesians chapters 2 and 3). This mystery, the Body of Believers, plays several functions in this world. We need to understand what the functions of the Body of Believers are in order to understand the mystery. You can see how sub-normal the life in the Body has been when you see these things.

First, the Body of Believers is to be a manifestation in this age of the Age to Come. We are to be a manifestation of the Kingdom, a manifestation of the Age to Come in this age. How does that happen? *The Kingdom is manifested by the gifts and the power of the Holy Spirit in us.* Paul says in Hebrews (if Paul wrote Hebrews) that we who have tasted of the Holy Spirit have tasted of the Age to Come. In the Age to Come, Israel and the nations will be one under the rule of the Messiah. In this age, Jew and Gentile are one under the rule of Messiah in the Body of Believers.

Second, the Body of Believers extends the Kingdom of God to all the nations. Those who respond before the very end of this age, before the awesome judgments and wrath of God are poured out, have the privilege to be part of the Bride. Jews and Gentiles who respond in this age will be the ruling queen by His side in the Age to Come.

Third, in extending the Kingdom to the nations, a people is formed in the midst of the earth who have the power in intercession and the power in witness to do what even the Apostles could not do - turn Israel back to Yeshua. Then all the prophecies of the Age to Come will be fulfilled. *That's the purpose of the Body - to preach and live the power and wholeness of the Gospel of the Kingdom as a witness to the entire world, and to make Israel jealous.* When we have fulfilled this task, Yeshua will return. It could be next year; I don't think so. It could be ten years. I'm not betting on it.

The role of the Body of Believers is not secondary in regard to the role of Israel. Many Christians are very upset with those who have an emphasis on Israel because they think it means that Christians are inferior. However, every believer is the spiritual seed of Abraham, raised with Him and seated with Him in heavenly places (Ephesians 2:6). The Body of Believers will be the ruling queen by His side in the Age to Come! There is no inferiority - ever! There is a call on Israel to be the capital nation in the midst of all the nations on earth in the Age to Come.

The purpose and meaning of the Body of Believers is rooted in Israel. God revealed this to the Apostles, but especially to Paul. James (Acts 15) got this revelation in part, that the Gospel was to be extended to the Gentiles. He quoted Amos 9 concerning the Age to Come, saying that if the Holy Spirit was poured out already, then why cannot Jew and Gentile become one as well, before the Age to Come arrives in fullness? Do you see what was going on there? They always saw the Body of Believers as something rooted in the meaning of Israel, not in the meaning of Rabbinic Judaism - Rabbinic Judaism is in error. The Body of Believers is something Jewish in roots, purpose and constitution.

THE COMMONWEALTH OF ISRAEL

The Apostles saw the Body of Believers as a commonwealth of Israel, not replacing the nation proper, but a commonwealth like the commonwealth of England. They saw that the commonwealth does not come to its place of completeness until the saved remnant of Israel is complete in number and until the nation itself turns back to God. Then in the Age to Come all the nations will make up the commonwealth of Israel, ruled by Yeshua and His queen - us! That's the total commonwealth that God is after.

Does the Church supersede Israel as in successionism? In other words, does the Church take Israel's place as God's people? Yes and no. **Yes, in the sense that we who are Yeshua's followers receive the fullness of covenantal benefit, and Israel now does not have the fullness of those protections.** Jews who do not believe in Yeshua are spoken of as broken off branches (Romans 11:17-24). **But also no, in the sense that Israel is still chosen, kept and preserved as broken branches.** Amazingly, there is not a complete replacement at all! Israel cannot be replaced, but Israel is still kept as God's chosen one unto her re-engrafting eventually into the one ultimate commonwealth of God, which the olive tree represents.[7] The commonwealth takes into account the whole thing. It takes into account the olive tree that Israel has to be grafted back into. **So, yes, the Body of Believers of Jew and Gentile is the place of primary covenant blessing, but Israel is preserved by Biblical promise and destined to that re-engrafting.**

By the end of the Second Temple Period[8], the Apostles had this understanding. They had an understanding of their role with Israel but they gave liberty to the Body of Believers. The Gentiles did not have to live a Jewish life. **The members of the commonwealth do not have to come under all aspects of the call and distinctions of the nation proper.** Acts 15 says that the nation proper is a pictorial manifestation by its Torah life of certain truths. The Gentiles were freed of the obligation to Jewish life but they were not freed from respect for Jewish practice and identity, which is a picture for their benefit. Having an understanding and respect for Jewish calling is Biblically assumed. In Acts 21, where the Jews are still zealous for the Law, there is no condemnation of them. But in Acts 15, the Gentiles are only enjoined to keep those parts of the law that are more universal. They don't have to live out the picture that Israel lives before the nations. If they want to, they can. Gentiles are free to join Jewish people in celebrations of the feasts and to observe with them.[9]

My perspective is that history is moving to bring the Body of Believers to a place of completeness and maturity whereby she will fulfill her role of making Israel jealous. Making Israel jealous is the capstone victory of the Body made up of the saved remnant of Israel and of the Gentiles. To accomplish this, the Gospel of the Kingdom has to be extended. The essential quality of the Body of Believers that must be present on earth, that can be visibly and understandably seen by Israel, must be a people that fulfill the John 17 prayer of Yeshua: "... that they might be one... that the world might believe..." We know that the world doesn't believe until the millennial age. The knowledge of the Lord will then cover the earth as the waters cover the sea (Isaiah 11).

Yeshua taught that the coming of the millennial age is related to the Body becoming one - one in maturity.[10] Yeshua said that they might be one **as You Father and I are one.** One in holiness. One in basic doctrine. Yeshua and the Father are not arguing over doctrine. There is a doctrinal foundation.

One person in the unity movement said, "Doctrine divides. Christ unites." What does that mean? Which Christ? As soon as you say the One who died and rose again, you've got doctrine! **If we are not united by the foundational doctrines of the Word of God, then we won't even know what we're talking about when we say the word "Messiah" or "Christ."**

The oneness that Yeshua prayed for is also related to the work of eldership. Paul in Ephesians 4:11-13 said that the five-fold ministry (apostles, prophets, pastors, evangelists, and teachers) will equip the saints for the work of the ministry **until we all come to the unity of the faith** (as in John 17) and to the knowledge of the Son of God. *The Body of Believers is called to be as a commonwealth of Israel, modeling the same kind of oneness among themselves that Christ modeled between Him and the Father. This will move Israel to jealousy and hasten the coming of Yeshua.*

---

4 Throughout this book the terms "Body of Believers" and "Church" will be used interchangeably.

5 The "Age to Come" refers to the time where all things in heaven and on earth are restored to their proper place and function. This will occur after Yeshua returns the second time to the earth to set up His physical earthly reign together with the Church, His Bride.

6 "Messiah" is a better term than "Christ" because it implies a kingly rule on David's throne. I don't think the term "Christ" conveys what

"Messiah" conveys – even in the English language. The word "Messiah" literally means *Anointed King, Ruler on David's throne*. Was "Christ" the divine side while "Jesus" was the human side? No. This is wrong theology, but that's how many Christians often think.

7 The olive tree will represent Israel and the nations saved in the Age to Come, in the millennial age. It represents the ruling queen by His side.

8 The end of the second Temple period is 70 A.D. when it was destroyed by Titus.

9 "Gentile" is not a pejorative or negative word. It is literally an abbreviation for nations – those from among all the nations. The word is used so Paul doesn't have to say, "I want to speak to you Frenchmen, Romans, Chinese, and Japanese." That would take too long. "Gentiles" is a way to abbreviate "the nations." In Romans Chapter 11 "Gentiles" means all other nations who God loves and wants to bring into the commonwealth in the Age to Come. Paul can say to Gentile believers, "I speak to you Gentiles" without any pejorative, negative prejudice.

10 Biblical unity is not the kind of unity that says, "Well, theology is unimportant; whatever you believe is fine. If you claim to speak in tongues, we're all together in unity. Well I know you left your wife for your secretary, but let's not allow that to hurt our unity!"

CHAPTER TWO

THE EARLY CHURCH - THE BEGINNING OF DECLINE

THE EARLY CHURCH - THE BEGINNING OF DECLINE

I look at the history of the church as a story of decline and restoration. I see so much church decline in this country that I have to really be walking by faith in God's Word and not by sight to believe in the restoration. In many cities of the United States the church is a mess. When the incidence of premarital sexual relations is only slightly less among our young people than the 73% in the secular world as a whole, we have major problems. We must raise our young people to walk in purity, remaining uninfluenced by the world. However, tragically the church has become "ghettoized" in her relationship to the world. She is not **in the world** like she is commanded to be, **but she is of the world like she is commanded not to be** - full of immorality and the seeking of self-centered personal peace and affluence. We've reversed the commandment to be in the world, but not of the world.

The church before the fall of Jerusalem was not a perfect church either. After the day of Pentecost, there was a brief period of very high unity and power in the church (Acts 2:42 ff.). The levels of carnality to be overcome are especially reflected in the epistles of Paul (see the Corinthian epistles). The prayer of

Yeshua in John 17 needed fulfillment in the first century as well as in our day. However, there were several features of the church **before the fall of Jerusalem** which were key aspects of what will be characteristic of the church that fulfills the prayer of Yeshua in John 17 and the teaching of Paul in Ephesians 4.

First, there was a basic unity of the church in every city. Whether a church of one hundred or a church of thousands, it was possible to address one church of every city. There was no competition among various denominations and streams in the Body of Believers. In the book of Revelation every church can be addressed as one church of each city. There might have been different meetings in different homes, but there was one true church. Contrary to writers today who warn against movements for church unity (and there is a real danger from sloppy movements of unity where right doctrine and behavior do not count for much), the apostles warn insistently against divisions and schism.

Second, the church before the fall of Jerusalem was in touch with Jewish roots. The Jerusalem church had a respect and leadership in the world of the church as a whole. The Apostles were Jewish. Therefore a Biblically rooted Jewish understanding of the meaning of Israel and the Church was normal. This will again be the case in the last-days Church. Apostolic doctrine united the church. So it will be of the last-days true Church (not the apostate church that will oppose the true Church). Whether justification by faith or the meaning of sanctification and faith, the last-days Church will be solid on apostolic doctrine.

Third, the first century church was familiar with the supernatural gifts of the Holy Spirit. The power of the Spirit was a normal experience in the life of the church. It was assumed as normative.

Therefore, Paul only needed to write correctives for using Holy Spirit gifts. The last-days Church will be strong in the use of the gifts of the Holy Spirit.

Fourth, the first century church, like the synagogue, was governed by a plurality of elders. Fivefold ministry was an expression of the ministry of the leaders of the Church (apostles, prophets, evangelists, pastors, and teachers). Likewise, we will see an expression of five-fold ministry and government by a mutually accountable eldership in each city and in every local congregational expression.

In my view the beginning of decline was the rejection of the Church's self-understanding with regards to Israel. I don't look at the decline as beginning with the loss of the gifts of the Holy Spirit in the second century, as some people who teach restoration believe. The supernatural gifts never disappeared completely. However there was a decline in the use of these gifts.[11]

THE CHURCH LOSES JEWISH ROOTS

Before the loss of the gifts of the Spirit there was an awesome rejection by the Gentile members of the Body of Believers of their Jewish roots. I believe that this was the real beginning of the decline. Why? **Because when Jerusalem fell, many Gentiles in the church took this to mean the final and open repudiation of Israel by God.** That fall and destruction of Jerusalem was great, both to Israel and to the Church. I want to be honest with you, the evidence for Church History right after 70 A. D. is not clear. S.G.F. Brandon, a scholar with whom I don't agree in many regards, however, accurately calls the period of 70 - 90 A. D. the tunnel period of New Testament history. It is the tunnel period because we have so little information for 20 years until the early writings of the Gentile church fathers. We do know that at the other end of that tunnel period, there was a great change in the church's understanding of Israel. All the Jewish Apostles were gone. Three great changes are discernable.

First, the destruction of Jerusalem and the scattering of many of the Jewish people was taken to be an ultimate and total repudiation of Israel. Many church leaders were judging by sight instead of by the Word.

Second, a tremendous love and identification with Greek and Hellenistic culture was suddenly introduced. In the second century and even more in the third, church fathers saw the writings of the Greek philosophers as almost equal to the Old Testament. Such Hellenistic writings were seen as preparatory revelation to the New Testament! You've got to read some of the fathers to see this. The early church fathers highly esteemed the works of Plato, Aristotle, and other Greek thinkers. Greek culture was something that they couldn't break from. There were, however, exceptions like Turtullian ("What has Jerusalem to do with Athens?").

Third, responses of the early church to severe persecution at the end of the first and early second century often alienated the church from Israel. We must appreciate the heroism of many of the believers from those days. Many died in martyrdom - some went to the lions. However, not all was favorable from our point of view. Some wanted to deny their connection to the Jewish people. Why? At first the Romans understood Christianity as a sect of Judaism. After the first revolt against Rome, the Jewish people were not a very favored people in the Roman Empire. Josephus' writings sought to remedy this situation. After they revolted again under Bar Kochba in the 130's, the Jewish people were even more despised.[12]

After the first revolt, there was still a significant Jewish population in the land of Israel. Earlier

Judaism had been given the status of a legitimate religion in the Roman Empire. The Jews in the empire were given a special legal privilege to not have to bow to the emperor and the idols of Rome in worship. They were the only exceptions. In the beginning the Christians wanted to be seen almost as Jews so that they would be a legitimate religion and not persecuted. However, after Israel lost its favor with Rome, to be identified with something Jewish was to add to the persecution. To the best of our information, there was a tremendous move in the church for people to identify themselves as good Roman citizens and Greek cultured people rather than to connect with Jewish roots.

Sunday, the Day of the Sun, became the day of worship. The Roman emperor in the 90's adopted the seven-day week. The church's day of worship became the first day of the week instead of the seventh day.[13] The Romans gave pagan names to the seven days of the week. We have the German version; Monday - Lunar Day; Tuesday - Mercury Day; Wednesday - Woden's Day; Thursday - Thor's Day. The church identified the light theme of the Day of the Sun with the light of the Son, S-O-N. This can be seen in the writings of the church fathers in the second century. However, there is no evidence that God intended to change the Sabbath day, at least not for Jews.

THE DENIAL OF THE SAVED REMNANT

The statement of Justin Martyr typifies the growing consensus to reject the legitimacy of the identity of the saved remnant of Israel. He said, "He who will be both Christian and Jew can be neither Christian nor Jew." Basically, Justin Martyr's statement was a denial of the saved remnant of Israel and its part both in the nation of Israel and in the Body of Believers. The "saved remnant of Israel" is both part of the Body of Believers universal and part of the nation of Israel. This is a very important theological concept. When Justin Martyr said, "He who would be both Christian and Jew can be neither Christian nor Jew," he first denied the legitimacy of the specific identity of Jewish life in Jesus. Additionally, he also expressed the denial of the continued role and future for national Israel. **I believe that this early rejection of the saved remnant planted the seed for the future persecution of the Jews by the church in later centuries, coming to fullness in the Holocaust.**

Many in the Christian community through the centuries have denied the saved remnant of Israel and identified with Greco-Roman roots over against Jewish roots. Instead of seeing the saved remnant of Israel as foundational, to which the rest of the Body is joined, and instead of encouraging an increase in that saved remnant, the church has often encouraged its isolation and decline.

In addition to the Christian community, the Jewish community also rejected the saved remnant of Israel as a legitimate part of Israel. They said they followed a false Messiah and were traitors because they didn't fight under Bar Kochba who was declared to be the Messiah by Rabbi Akiba (in the 130's). The saved remnant of Israel declined to a small number by the end of the second century, and declined to almost non-existence by the sixth century. Probably the seventh century onslaught of Islam wiped out the last remnants of the saved remnant of Israel, as far as we can determine. Believing Jews were forcibly converted to Islam. Today there are Arab villages that have symbols that probably imply that some of its people are descendants of the saved remnant of Israel.

Therefore, as we seek to understand the beginning of decline in the Early Church, we must understand the importance of the saved remnant of Israel. If the Church desires to see the restoration of New Testament truth she must be sure that she is standing on the right foundation - the foundation of accepting, embracing, and rightly joining with the saved remnant of Israel.

11 The gifts are the graces of the Holy Spirit whereby the Holy spirit is powerfully present. The gracelets or gifts are types of empowerment provided by God for what we are called to do. I think that if you study the meaning of the term "Holy Spirit" in first century Judaism, you will find that where the Holy Spirit is present to a significant extent, there are manifestations of the Holy Spirit. Holy Spirit power and Holy Spirit manifestation were indistinguishable from one another in the first century mind and were not easily separable. When you have one you have the other. It is only in later Greek influenced thinking that one tries to divide the two.

12 Most Christians know little or nothing about the second revolt.

13 I believe the Resurrection occurred on the first day of the week. I know some argue in the Messianic Movement that it occurred on Shabbat, but I think the logical conclusion from Scripture is to rest on the seventh day. The first day is creation, the Feast of Firstfruits and the feast of resurrection.

CHAPTER THREE

THE BEGINNING OF
THE CATHOLIC CHURCH

ONE PEOPLE MANY TRIBES

THE BEGINNING OF THE CATHOLIC CHURCH: CONSEQUENCES IN THE CHURCH FOR REJECTING HER JEWISH ROOTS

What happens when the church denies its Jewish roots? **The church can no longer understand theology with accuracy.** The Bible says in Romans 3:1 concerning the Jews, "What advantage is there in being a Jew? Much in every way; they are given the very words of God." One of the gifts given to the Jewish people is **revelation and interpretation** of God's Word. There were many, many declines that take place in the third century, perhaps as a result of this repudiation of Jewish believers. Even though the Holy Spirit was still working in the church at this time, the church now understood church government from a different point of view. The Apostles, I believe, understood congregational government as vested in a plurality of elders, as in the synagogue. The term "elder" was the same used to refer to the elders of the gate in ancient Israel. During the early years of Israel's nationhood, judges always functioned in the context of plurality; however, among this plurality specific judges would rise to prominence to lead the other judges. It was natural. So it was in the synagogue.

The plurality of elders in the first century synagogue was parallel to the structure of government of the plurality of judges in the cities of ancient Israel. The church however, was looking to Greco-Roman models for its self-understanding. Not only were its **theological concepts defined in Greek terms** rather than Jewish functional terms, but the church understood its **government in Roman terms.** It patterned its structure of government and hierarchy after the Roman models of government. The functions of church governmental officials were exactly parallel in authority and extent to Roman governmental boundaries and governmental positions. The pope was parallel to the emperor when Rome was defined as the most prominent bishopric (Pontifix-Maximus). The term "Pontiff" is derived from Roman government. The bishop became parallel to the ruler of a city in the empire. Where was Israel in all this? Where are Jewish models? Nowhere! This is decline.

Parallel to this decline is the loss of the gifts of the Holy Spirit. A theology developed to affirm this loss as intended by God. Augustine in the fifth century codified both declines as not being declines! Augustine taught that there was no future for the Jewish people, but that they were preserved to be an example of what happens to a people who reject God. Augustine said that they would never again enter their land; they would never again enter God's favor because they crucified the Messiah - God. Augustine also explained that the gifts of the Spirit were only intended for the purpose of testifying to the authority of the apostolic leaders of the first century.[14] Protestant theology followed Augustine's earlier views on the gifts.

THE WORK OF GOD IN THE PATRISTIC[15] CHURCH

It is important that in giving such a simple summary we avoid an error. This would be to think that the Spirit of God was not working in the church in spite of decline. It is not as though all aspects of the church were in decline. Indeed progress was made on some fronts while decline is seen on other fronts. The church produced amazing and godly leaders such as Ambrose and Cyprian. We need to avoid the error of thinking that, despite an over emphasis on Greek thinking, all their conceptions were wrong. In addition, we need to recognize that Greek modes of thinking provide helpful perspectives as well, as long as the original Hebraic context is kept in mind. This is true for many languages, but we must especially ask why God saw fit to see the New Covenant revelation in the Greek language.

The patristic leaders (early church fathers) faced many challenges. Great varieties of views battled for supremacy among Christians. This included eastern religious influences through a culture called *Gnostacism*[16]. To battle these tendencies, the church gathered its leaders to define its faith against these foreign influences. In an effort to safeguard the church, the office of the bishop was created. While following Roman models of the government of a city, the bishop became a key to safeguarding the truth of the church. It appears from the writings of the Ante-Nicene Fathers that the bishop was originally the *first among equals* in the council (which was the presbytery - the elders of the city who made decisions in the context of plurality).

By the end of the second century, the bishop functioned as the decision making head, the "Monarchical Bishop" as he came to be known. Although Bishop Victor of Rome, at the end of the second century, asserted his supremacy over all other bishops, the Eastern bishops did not accept this and from that day until now still maintain the plurality concept of government at the level of bishop.

Councils of bishops defined our basic doctrines of the nature of God, the nature of Yeshua as

human and divine and other aspects of doctrine. While the conceptions would be seen by Messianic Jews as overly Greek, I believe that the Spirit of God worked in spite of a lack of appreciation for Jewish roots.[17] **Nicea**, in 325 A. D. defined the Triune nature of God as one God eternally existent in three persons, equal in essence as divinity but not co-equal in function. **Chalcedon**, in 451 A. D. gave us the conception of Yeshua as one person with both a divine and human nature. Yeshua after the pre-existent Messiah's incarnation is fully human and fully divine.

Unifying the church in basic doctrine was no small task. The understanding of Nicea and Chalcedon has been affirmed by evangelicals to our day. These statements of doctrine were put in creedal statements recited by many in historic denominations. The church did over compromise with Greek philosophy, yet nevertheless it did repel the dangerous errors levied by Gnostic and pagan attacks. The church was not perfect in this by any means, but was greatly successful.

It is not as though the history of the church did not continue to produce advance even during the Middle Ages. Pious missionaries who truly loved the Lord spread the Gospel to many lands. Patrick to Ireland was typical of the best. Doctrinal progress was made in some areas. For example, in the 12th century, St. Anselm first clearly put forth the theology of the death of Yeshua for our sins as a substitutionary satisfaction. It is amazing that others before him did not penetrate New Testament thinking before he did. His view became the standard Catholic view through Thomas Aquinas and through the reformers in the 16th century.

JEWISH ROOTS AND SPIRITUAL POWER

Didn't the Apostles offer Israel repentance after

the crucifixion? **Israel's scattering is not based on the crucifixion.** It was her failure to receive the **benefits** of the crucifixion. Instead, she received the judgement. It was a failure to respond to the apostolic witness in signs and wonders. Under the umbrella of apostolic authority and teaching, covenantal blessing and protection were to be found. Under apostolic doctrine the promise of blessing continues. Israel's preservation and scattering, even in persecution, shows forth covenantal dimensions. Augustine said no to this view. Augustine also looked at the absence of the gifts of the Holy Spirit and said they were for the purpose of getting things started.[18] The power of the signs and wonders and manifestations of the Kingdom in the New Testament become re-interpreted to mean, "these things happened so that the Apostles' authority would be accepted. These things were only needed before the Scriptures were written. These things were attestations of the divinity of Yeshua and have nothing to do with the fact of our being filled with the Spirit. Experiencing the Spirit in this way was only for the special saints."

Were the miracles, signs and wonders really attestations to His *divinity*, or were they more attestations to His being *filled with the power of the Spirit*? Scripture's testimony is that He didn't draw from His own divinity. He could have. He could have called for the twelve legions of angels to avoid the cross. But to be the perfect example for us He lived as a human being filled with the power of the Holy Spirit. In Him we see the potential of a man filled with the Holy Spirit. We will never fully attain His perfection and power, but we can reach our potential in Him and be more and more like Him.

How do you approach the Scriptures? A tradition grew up that still has a very big hold on the Body. It is called *cessationism*, claiming that the gifts, power, and manifestations of the Holy Spirit seen in the New

Testament were meant to cease. I believe that this doctrine is related to the rejection of a Jewish understanding of the Holy Spirit, which is clearly found in Jewish sources, and is also found as a central aspect of understanding the Biblically Jewish roots of our Christianity.

Judaism had its own Greek influence upon it; one can see tremendous Greek influence in the Talmud. I believe that Yeshua's battle with the religious leaders was in part a battle with Hellenism in Judaism. **Hellenism turned Judaism toward a rationalistic orientation.** We cannot underestimate the awesome influence of the Hellenistic world both on them and on us.[19]

Something contrary to Jewish thinking began to happen. A doctrine was developed in the church that was totally un-Jewish. Think of Jewish context and life. *A primary Jewish truth was that all men are responsible before God and should be able to read the synagogue scrolls for themselves and teach the Word to their children.* Every Jew, especially a Jewish man, was expected to know how to read, how to write, and how to understand the scrolls.

In the church, because of Gentile hierarchical perspectives, the laity could become illiterate. Much emphasis was placed on the teaching ministry of the church, and the people were expected to follow their leaders. They were to believe what they were told without questioning authority. The knowledge of the Word of God was lost. The ideal of the masses knowing the Word was lost.[20] They lost the Jewish-rooted understanding that if you are going to have the Torah, and the Torah is the foundation of revelation, then everyone needs to know the Torah. Historical evidence strongly suggests that most Jewish young men, at the time of Yeshua, understood and memorized the whole Torah, the Psalms and many parts of the Prophets. This was accomplished by the time they were bar mitzvah age (13 years old). The conviction that we must understand the Word of God began to fade.

After Rome fell, the Dark Ages came. This was not a totally dark age, but there was a significant loss of learning. **The loss of the knowledge of the Word of God facilitated the acceptance of false doctrines.** Works became joined to justification as being necessary for salvation as opposed to good works done in faith as being the fruit of justification.[21] Undeserved grace is what enables us to first believe and to receive the Lordship of Yeshua into our lives. The idea of works and indulgences (purchasing the release of loved ones from purgatory) and all of the things that we know in the decline of Catholicism are connected to the loss of the Word of God. Hierarchy, the ignorance of the masses, and forced conversions; **the decline was massive.**

There is a decline when people who claim to be Christians hold forth their swords and say, "Believe and be baptized!" There is a decline when you believe that there is a purgatory and that people can be purchased out of it by giving gifts to the church. There is a decline when many priests cannot even read. There is a decline when clergy live in sumptuous luxury. Cardinal Woolsey, at the beginning of the 16th century, had a bigger palace than King Henry VIII. He was in danger for his life because King Henry was jealous. Cardinal Woolsey had to donate his palace to Henry. There is nothing new under the sun. Today some wealthy ministers in the church think like this: "Well, I have a big ministry. A big ministry has the same responsibilities as does a corporate manager, so I should live like the president of GM." This is not new thinking! What was Cardinal Woolsey thinking? "I am head of the Roman Catholic Church of England. The church is even more important and glorious than the civil state, so I should live at least as well as King Henry VIII." The late Jamie Buckingham put it this way: "At a certain point we lose touch with reality."[22]

Were there any real believers during medieval Catholicism? I think that Francis of Assisi was saved. There were movements to purify the church, including monastic movements, which partially restored some truths. I've read Francis of Assisi's writings and he believed some strange things too. St. Francis, however, did show kindness to Jewish people.

Another tremendous decline was in the lack of purity in the lives of believers. The church was full of immorality. The priests and congregants alike were steeped in immorality. Yet they were paying indulgences to get people out of purgatory. The church was full of superstition too. When you convert masses by the sword, their paganism is still part of their identity. Magic and paganism were still maintained within the European tribal situation after the church conquered these various peoples. Things got very dark.

Remember, I believe that the decline began with the rejection of Jewish roots. We always have a decline when we fail to honor our fathers and mothers. Even parents that are the worst parents have at least preserved the life of their child. Without them the child wouldn't exist. Even in the worst parenting situation there is something for which to say, "Thank you God." There is always something for which to honor our parents.[23]

Rightly honoring one's parents is also a corporate principle as well. Israel is the parent of the Church, though a wayward parent - a parent that did not submit to God. The saved remnant did. Israel can also see the Church as a very wayward child! **The Church's response to Israel has been very similar to the proud child who accepts the Lord and is arrogant against their unbelieving parents.** By the same token, the Charismatic Movement, in being arrogant against the denominations, has become anarchistic and chaotic, even though the denominations gave birth to everything that is happening today. I am not a super-denominationalist, as you will see when we come to the end of this.

Thus, it was in the beginnings of the Catholic Church that we can see tragic consequences in the Body of Believers resulting from a rejection of her Jewish roots. Primary, was the paradigm shift of a Hebraic context of God, man, and government to a more Hellenistic rational context which ultimately resulted in a denial of the Church's Biblically Jewish roots. The restoration of truth is most definitely also a restoration of proper roots.

14 Augustine in his later life discovered real miracles and gifts and then changed on this point as noted in the writing of William Artega in *Quenching The Spirit*.

15 The Patristic period is the period of the church fathers in the early centuries of the era after the apostolic period extending up to the time of Augustine.

16 Gnosticism was an ancient heretical religious belief system that emphasized a strong distinction between the material world and the spiritual world. They believed that humans were confined to the material world and were unable to ascend into the superior world of the spirit without special revelation (*gnosis*). Thus, secret knowledge marked Gnosticism as the only hope for people to be freed from the confines of the material world. As such, Gnosticism was strongly opposed to Christianity because it affirmed a salvation rooted in a "hidden knowledge" rahter than the person and work of Yeshua.

17 Oscar Skarsone of the Free Lutheran Theological faculty in Oslo, Norway, has written extensively on this. He is an expert in early Jewish Christianity and Patristics. His argument is very forceful that the conceptions of Nicea and Chalcedon were basically correct if the Greek language was to be used. His book, *Incarnation, Myth or Fact* is a key book on this subject.

18 Often people develop their theology to defend their experience. They want to feel okay. They want to feel that where they are in life is fine so

they rationalise their beliefs through a well developed theology. Augustine was a very great man of God in many ways. However, when he saw the powerlessness of the Church and political power replacing real spiritual power he theologized it as the way God intended it to be. Instead of the Church getting on its knees and saying, "O God! What's happened to us? We're not like the apostolic beginnings. Where have we gone wrong? Show us how to change so that we can be restored to Your power," theology grew up that said, "This is the way that it is supposed to be."

19 The Hellenistic world is not all bad. There are certain dimensions of truth from Noah and from natural revelation that are found in Hellenistic culture. But there's a lot that is not good. Hellenistic-Roman culture affected most people in that particular stage of history.

20 The authority of leadership is to help us understand and interpret the Word. Though this is an important function, it is not absolute. The check on that authority is that we are to read the Word to make sure our leaders are not going into doctrinal error. However, when the masses are not allowed to know the Bible for themselves, then a very important "safety net" is cut away from them.

21 Works should never be seen as ways to gain God's favor. We are saved only by faith through grace. *Grace is the enabling power of obedience.* Yet, I don't want to go to the other side to what I consider the heresy of J.N. Darby. This heresy teaches that we can be saved and continue to live in sin. Grace is always the empowerment of the Holy Spirit to obey.

22 I do believe in **Biblical** propserity. I'm wearing a new suit today and this is the first time I've worn it. This suit was a gift from the Korean Christians ... a tailor made it. I feel quite prosperous. I am not against prosperity. I don't believe I should come here in shredded garments and a hair shirt, which is the other aberration, asceticism. Asceticism is the pummleing of the body, having the stigmata, living in poverty as a sign of piety. This is an unhealthy extreme too.

23 If you fail to honor your parents, instead of receiving the good from them and having an accurate understanding of the bad, you will repeat the wrong patterns in your own life through the sin of bitterness. You will fail to receive the good heritage from your parents.

CHAPTER FOUR
THE REFORMATION

THE REFORMATION

Into this darkness came the Reformation. When evil comes in like a flood, the Lord promises that He will raise up a standard. The Lord was never without a witness. There were the pre-Reformers, Huss and Wycliff, as well as pious believers in the Catholic Church that remained faithful. Yet, things became so dark that today it is hard to imagine just how bad it was. By the time of the Reformation, there was a loss in the understanding of Biblical Jewish roots, Biblical unity, five fold ministry, government by a plurality of elders locally and in each city, the gifts of the Holy Spirit among the people, Scriptural authority, and justification by faith.

REFORMATION UNDER LUTHER

During this time a young priest in the Catholic Church was wrestling with anxiety in his heart; his name was Martin Luther. He could not get peace with God through the disciplines of asceticism or other disciplines. The superstitions that had become Catholic doctrine were not working.[24]

Luther did something at the risk of his life; he nailed 95 theses on the Wittenberg Church door. Luther came to the light of the 95 Theses only through the revelation of the Holy Spirit. The 95 Theses were a dramatic and accurate statement of evangelical Biblical truth. That he could come to that understanding in the midst of the darkness of the times was amazing. That he took the courageous step to nail it on the door of the church to seek to bring reformation to the Catholic Church was also amazing. **Luther did not want to leave the Catholic Church yet through this stand of conviction he did get kicked out.** This was not his original intention. He wanted a return to the doctrine of justification by faith and a return to the authority of the Word of God. He saw the need for the laity, as well as the clergy, to be educated.

Luther also committed an act that was considered a great heresy of practice. He translated the Bible into the German tongue so that the people could read it. Gutenberg was largely motivated in inventing the printing press so that the Bible could be read by the people. The Reformers all saw the necessity to educate the people. Universal education became a goal so that the people could read the Word of God.

When I think of how God brings light in the midst of darkness, I get a little bit shaky. Luther committed some terrible sins, but he was a great man. This is the case despite his coarse language and despite the anti-Semitism of his later years. He lived in the midst of a culture that was anti-Semitic and received the tradition of the rejection of Israel. God's restoration is progressive.

There was a price on his head, a judgment of death. The church was not able to stop the fire that Luther lit. He was given safe passage by King Charles V to come to a Diet to defend himself before a council of the church. Johann Eck was the prosecutor. King Charles promised Luther that after the meeting he would be given safe passage to the territory of the princes who supported him. Here, people had become either convinced of the doctrines of the Reformation or they merely had a desire to lessen the power of the Papacy.

I have a doctrine that great people can do great good and great evil. For example, the German people are a great people and have produced tremendous good for the world, and yet have been instruments of tremendous evil. Because capacity is capacity, it can be used for good or evil. This is true of Luther as well.

Luther stood before that council at Worms. He did not know if Charles would keep his word (kings didn't always keep their word). Church officials could have said, "We supersede Charles' word and command it to be null and void. We command the arrest of Luther." He went to defend the authority of the Scriptures and the doctrine of justification by faith. He risked his life. He stood before the council and answered the accusations. He was asked by John Eck, "How can you, Martin, stand against princes and kings, church councils and popes, and all that they have taught through the years, and exalt yourself in arrogance (and I'm paraphrasing) against the Catholic Church?" Luther looked out at the gathering and said, **"Whether there be councils, they have erred; whether there have been popes, they have sinned and gone astray; if anyone shall show me by Scripture that anything I teach is in error, I will repent. But until I am shown by Scripture that I am wrong, my conscience is captive to the Word of God."** Some historians say that he then said, **"Here I stand; I can do no other."**

It is hard for me to keep my composure when I recount the story of Luther. I have never been able to retell it without tears. It is even more poignant in terms of sadness when we understand what happened in his later life. He was not a light to the Jewish people as the Lord commanded us all to be. Can we see that this man, who later became anti-Semitic when Jews failed to respond to the Gospel during the Reformation, performed one of the most courageous acts of all history? Without it, I don't believe we would be here today with our theology and understanding that we do have. I don't even believe the Messianic Jewish Movement would exist. What an extraordinary paradox we live with!

Incredibly, the king kept his word. Luther was given safe passage. However, afterwards, he was hunted from place to place until the day he died. He died young, in part because of the tremendous attack against him and its consequent anxiety. Maybe that was partly why he was so irascible. He did not display all of the fruits of Spirit in great measure; however, he did show one great fruit - **courage.**

The great restoration truths in Luther were justification by faith and the authority of Scripture. On the question of the relationship between *Law* and *Grace*, Luther was inconsistent. Sometimes he was accurate on one page and then on another page he would write something strange and not in agreement with what he had previously written. Luther was a brilliant creative theologian, but not a consistent theologian. Justification by faith and the authority of the Scripture for testing doctrine, *sola Scriptura* - these were the great things to come out of Luther. But Lutheranism was not the epitome of full restoration. Jewish people looked at the Lutheran church and **did not see Jewish roots restored.** This is partly because Jewish people identify Jewish roots with rabbinical Judaism.

In the process of restoration, often what was first to be lost is last to be restored. There are glimmers of restoration truth in all dimensions throughout history. There isn't a neat pattern or an easy logical progression throughout history of step by step restoration of what was lost. The Reformation unleashed something upon the world that was wonderful, but the prophets of the Reformation also produced fragmentation. The beginnings of fragmentation were not large. Fragmentation came as people were reading the Word of God and trying to understand it afresh. They did not have the presence of the Apostles to help. Nor did they have an adequate Jewish context for understanding.

The Jewish roots context is very important for the sake of the unity of the church.[25] The people seeking truth had the Holy Spirit but there was still pride and vested interest within the Reformation as well. People began to read the Bible differently and came to various truths for restoration. There was not the humility and patience to stay together and pray toward unity and agreement, yet the Reformers taught that schism was a serious sin. Maintaining the unity of the church was still a high ideal, but not at the price of truth. However, in restoration we need to listen and learn and not be quick to condemn if we are to find this unity. We need patience within evangelical orthodoxy to allow God to accomplish His purposes.

THE EASTERN ORTHODOX CHURCH

At the time of the Reformation there were two churches. One was the Eastern Orthodox Church and the other was the Western Roman Catholic Church. The split had come some hundreds of years earlier. The Eastern church itself was a church in decline. One of the reasons for the split in Eastern Orthodoxy relates to the repudiation of Jewish Biblical roots. Although Eastern Orthodoxy also became anti-Semitic and Replacement in orientation, they did see themselves as rooted in a Jewish calendar and Jewish things more than the Western church. Nevertheless, they too still had their own version of the repudiation of Jewish roots.

One of the controversies between East and West

went back to the second century. It was over whether the Jewish calendar or the Roman solar calendar was to be used for the dating of Christian feasts. The Eastern church, especially with regard to Passover and the Resurrection, kept the Jewish calendar. This was not the only reason for the split some 800 years later. There were political issues and the issue of the authority claimed by the Roman Catholic Church.[26]

In the second century the pope of Rome, Victor, argued with the Bishop of Antioch, Polycrates. Polycrates wrote to Victor and argued, "How can you demand that the whole Christian world keep the Roman calendar for the celebration of Easter when we have it directly from the Apostles to celebrate the death and resurrection of Yeshua, according to the Jewish calendar, on the 14th of Nisan?" Originally the government of the church was vested in a plurality of elders. However, what began as a plurality of elders with a head elder (bishop) over each city evolved into the monarchical bishop over each city. The plurality of bishops together as a council over churches evolved to the primacy of the Roman bishop. This primacy of the Roman See doctrine was later rejected by the Eastern church, as manifested in the 11th century split from Rome.

Eastern Orthodox people believed that they, not the Roman Church, were the true apostolic Church. The Orthodox churches still maintain authority in patriarchs. They also hold to several doctrines that are troubling to Messianic Jews, such as the veneration of saints, worship through icons, and acetic practices.

THE REFORMATION UNDER CALVIN

The light of the Reformation spread to different countries. Most noteworthy was the Reformed Movement in Europe and the Anabaptists movement. I want to talk about Reformed understanding. John Calvin was inspired by Luther and was a man of significant courage. Calvin, in seeking to be true to Scripture, wrote *The Institutes of the Christian Religion*.[27]

The Calvinist Reformation in France and Switzerland later spread to Holland, England, and Scotland. In England and Scotland it was called "Presbyterianism," meaning, "government by elders." Calvin talked about the church being reformed and always reforming. This is an interesting thought because what often times happens when truth is restored is that a people gather around that truth and around a particular leadership figure.[28]

Calvin's view of restoration believed that our knowledge of truth is partial and forever in need of greater reformation. We know in part, as the Apostle Paul said. However, the Reformed Movement didn't always practice that! Calvin's writings became the epitome of truth, and no man in the process of discovering restoration truth is the epitome. There was a lot more in these older writers that many think wasn't restored until recently. The amount of truth they had perceived amazes many today. However, I am absolutely amazed at the amount of truth perceived by many of these older writers like Calvin. We often think much of the restoration truths we have come to know in modern times were recent restorations, but much of it was already unveiled through the writings of such men in the history of the church.

Calvin is usually known for his doctrine of predestination, known by the famous acronym: T - U - L - I - P. This stands for "**T**otal depravity, **U**nconditional election, **L**imited atonement, **I**rresistible grace, and the **P**erseverance of the saints." I was in the Reformed church of America when I was a teenager and received the Lord. I first prayed to receive the Lord after the preaching of a guest speaker named George Sweeting, a recent president of Moody Bible Institute, who at that time was the pastor of the Madison Avenue Baptist Church in Patterson, New Jersey. He was preaching in our Dutch Reformed church, which was at that time premillennial! Shortly after Sweeting's visit, the pastor of our church retired and was replaced by one who was a more traditional Reformed amillennialist.[29] I remember one time when I was in high school and he said, "O, brethren, let us hold onto this wonderful truth: whom God wills to save, He saves; and whom He wills to damn, He damns." Many people think, "Well, that's Calvinism." However, that is only one part of it. To me it is a shame that Calvinism, and the Reformed Movement, got identified with a rigid predestinarianism that in some Calvinists led to fatalism. However, Calvinism was restoring so much more than that.

I believe that the primary restoration that took place under Calvinism was two fold. **First, it was an understanding of the Biblical government in the church as vested in a plurality of elders.** This was much more akin to the first century synagogue government and I believe that this was the government of the first century Messianic congregations. Right government is a very important reality for the church to understand.

The second thing that was restored in Calvinism was a significant understanding of the Kingdom of God. It was not the full understanding. More complete understandings are put forth in the writings of Abraham Kuyper, the prime minister of Holland at the turn of the century. In recent times, George Ladd of Fuller Seminary put forth an even more excellent perspective on this. I haven't found anything better to this date.[30] The beginnings of true Kingdom understanding, however, were found in John Calvin.

Sometimes the Kingdom of God was identified in Catholic thought as the institutional church per se. The Catholic Church understood the Kingdom of God as the Roman ecclesiastical organization. Although you can see this idea to some extent in Calvin, there is a moving away from this identification to a more Biblical understanding **that the Kingdom is seen in every realm where people submit to the rule of God.** Calvin understood that the church preaches the Gospel of the Kingdom. The Good News is an invitation to come under the rule of the King through the atonement of Yeshua. It is not the weak doctrine of grace taught in many of today's churches, but a doctrine that includes grace for obedience. Biblical grace always carries the sense of empowerment to obedience.

Calvin also had a high regard for the Law. He understood that believers were not under the Mosaic Covenant, but that the moral teachings of the whole Bible are enjoined as instruction to train us in righteousness (II Timothy 3:16, 17). Luther did not have as clear an understanding, in my view, of the purpose of the Law in instructing and discipling the believer as did Calvin. Calvin taught that the moral teachings of the Law do not have to be repeated in the New Testament to be enjoined. I think that Calvin had a weak delineation in contrasting the moral law and the ceremonial law. It is not as easy to distinguish as Calvin thought. We need to, in the Spirit, approach the teaching of Moses and ask, "How does each command apply in the New Covenantal order?" "What is the Lord writing on my heart?" Calvinists understood that antinomianism, or "anti-lawism" is a dangerous plague. Calvin did basically understand law and grace correctly.

Calvin also taught a brilliant doctrine of vocation. This is a great restoration truth. Every believer has a vocation and does not have to be a full-time preacher. His vocation may be a ruler in civil government, an artist, an educator, an artisan, or an inventor. **All legitimate vocations were equally callings of God. People were called to manifest the glory of God in their various vocations. All vocational calls were glorious and justified by God. God wants to manifest the principles of His Kingdom rule in all of the different realms of life.** The businessman shows the Kingdom of God in the way he runs and does his business. It is the same with the artist, the scientist, and the builder. The Calvinist conceptions of culture in their varieties within the history of Calvinism, are brilliant. This led to the understanding that it is not only full-time ministers who are to govern the churches. People in other vocations can be equally spiritual and can come into eldership to be leaders in the church. The government of the church became open to laity. Just think of it! For its time, this was revolutionary.

These were great restorations of truth in Calvinism, but did Calvin really understand Israel? No. Did Luther understand Israel? No. Did they tend toward replacement theology? Yes. Did Calvin understand the millennial age, that there would be a literal millennium? No. Did Luther? No. They still accepted the Catholic understanding of those things. There was still more truth to be restored.

24 I am not anti-Catholic. There are saved cathoilcs and today many Cathoilcs embrace some of Martin Luther's corrections.

25 The context of Jewish roots is the only context able to release Biblical unity to all areas of the church in both understanding and experience. Every other attempt will eventually become a schism. Wherever unity is dealy with, the root is what must always be addressed.

26 When we think of the fact that the mode of time measure known as a week of seven days did not exist outside of world Jewry in the first century, we can understand and are empathetic to the practice of taking Roman

calendar days and using them to celebrate Christian meanings that are parallel to pagan misconceptions. Christians would be given these days off like other Romans but would not be allowed to take Jewish days off. However, in using Roman holidays as times for Christian celebration, the church should have acknowledged the Biblical holy days as the original context for New Covenant meanings. This is proper cultural adaption.

27 It is almost hard to believe that he could have written something that was so doctrinally adequate in the midst of the world at that time. He wrote it when he was only twenty-six years old, though he significantly revised it over the following years of his life. There is a light and a brilliance in *The Institutes* that is trluy astonishing.

28 Theses figures might be seen as apostolic figures with a small "a." If you belive in five-fold ministry, Luther was apostolic in terms of what he was and did. But this is small "a" apostle. You will never have the Apostles again, like the Biblical Apostles that wrote Scripture and were eyewitnesses to Yeshua. You do have people that lead movements, oversee congregations, or plant multiple congregations. People tend to camp around the truth that is restored and don't go on to further restoration. The reverence given to the founding leader is often too great. His teaching becomes almost on a par with Scripture.

29 The belief that the millennium (the 1,000 year reign of Yeshua and the saints ruling with Him) is not a future event yet to come, but is a present historical reality already happening. The 1,000 year reign of believers is understood as having begun with the completed work of Yeshua on the cross and the "1,000 years" actually means an undesignated amount of time spanning from the Cross to the Second coming of Yeshua.

30 *The Gospel of the Kingdom*, by George Eldon Ladd

CHAPTER FIVE
THE ANABAPTISTS

THE ANABAPTISTS

The Anabaptists believed that the Reformation did not go far enough.[31] There were two changes from Calvinism implemented in Anabaptist theology. One's theology will determine whether or not one believes that these changes are a restoration of truth. The Anabaptists - not to be confused with the Baptist church, which is an offshoot of Puritanism - are the people we know today as the Mennonites, the Amish, the Church of the Brethren, and the Peace Churches.

First, the Anabaptists believed that infant baptism was not legitimate and taught that baptism was to be by immersion for believing adults only. I believe that baptism by immersion is one of the restorations that came through the Anabaptists (and later the Puritan Baptists). If you are a Presbyterian or a Lutheran you may not think that this was a restoration.

Second, the Anabaptists had a different understanding of culture. The Calvinist understanding of culture was to bring the rule of God into every area of life. **The Anabaptists believed that the society was so corrupt that they had to create a total counter culture and be disengaged from society.**

The Reformed view emphasized invasion of every sector of life by the Gospel message; the Anabaptist view was to create an alternative society. The Anabaptists formed Peace Churches and were pacifists. They did not believe, according to their interpretation of the Sermon on the Mount, that it was ever right for believers to go to war. You can ask whether that was a higher restoration or not.

My own view with regards to the Anabaptists and the Reformed view of engaging culture, is that there is a creative tension between the two. The stance the church takes — whether the Anabaptist stance or the Reformed — is circumstantial. I believe that in the United States, historically and at the present time, the Reformed stance is the right one for the church. We may be soon forced into the Anabaptist stance, at least for a time, to purify the church. The institutions of culture may become so corrupt that we cannot involve ourselves in them to influence them without ourselves becoming corrupt. The world is too much in the church.

The Reformed and the Anabaptist views are both right, depending upon the circumstances that you find yourself in. If you can invade the structures and change them by the leading of the Holy Spirit, then do so. You can be politically involved. If under the Spirit you can take over educational structures and demonstrate the Kingdom's principles, you should do it. There must be sufficient numbers to support these efforts. Such efforts must always be in conjunction with evangelism as they serve to be a part of our Christian witness. Evangelism must always be foremost in priority.

If you cannot invade the structures of society without destroying your families, your lives, and the churches, then be more Anabaptistic. When there are enough believers living in holiness and love, then the culture can be influenced by their strength of witness. The Anabaptists created their own culture apart from the rest of society. Anabaptist societies are not the total ideal. The Amish became more of a works-righteousness society. Today, most believers whom I have spoken to, who live in Amish country, say that the Amish do not understand justification by faith. The Mennonites do!

One of the glories of the Mennonites is that their pacifist position kept them from persecuting Israel. **The Mennonites were the first movement of Christians, institutionally, that did not persecute the Jewish people.** That does not mean that there was not some anti-Semitism in conception, but their understanding of the way of treating people in love was such that you can't find, to my knowledge, any incidence of Anabaptist persecution of the Jewish people.

The Anabaptist understanding of Christ and culture has become one of the most primary issues of interpretation that distinguish the different Anabaptist movements. Certainly, as we seek a greater restoration of Biblical truth in the Church today we must continue to wrestle with this important issue.

---

31 Anabaptist means *to baptize again*.

CHAPTER SIX
THE ANGLICAN CHURCH

THE ANGLICAN CHURCH
- A BRIEF SUMMARY

The Reformed Movement came into England. Lutheran and Reformed theology influenced the Anglican church. King Henry VIII did not want to be under the Catholic Church because he wanted to behead wives that didn't produce a male heir. King Henry was an interesting figure. He broke from the Catholic Church, probably not because he believed in Reformation teachings, but because it was political and expedient for his moral choices.

The evangelical Anglicans did really want a separation from the Roman Catholic Church for spiritual reasons. The Anglicans put Lutheran, Reformed, and Catholic understandings together. The Anglicans believed in Apostolic Succession[32] and the hierarchy of bishops. We need to allow the doctrine of Apostolic Succession to challenge us to question the extreme position in American Christianity where people appoint themselves to leadership and then claim God's call. However, should not real elders ordain new elders? In general does this not trace back to the apostolic ordination of elders? **There is no warrant in Scripture for self appointment to leadership and non-accountability.**

Anglo-Catholics maintained a Catholic view of

the Lord's Supper, which is called transubstantiation (this belief affirms that the elements really are the literal body and blood of Yeshua). Anglicans held to the Lutheran doctrine of justification by faith but were closer to the Reformed Calvinist view on some other issues. The 39 Articles are a very important statement of doctrine for the church.[33] When the Reformed Movement came to England, the first reported moves of the Holy Spirit with significant manifestations were among the protestants in England.

In their pursuit of Biblical truth, the evangelical Anglicans were those able to sift key Biblical truths from a variety of traditions and movements. Though their pursuits required difficult choices God honored them with a fresh release of His presence.

[32] Apostolic Succession is the doctrine that the Apostles passed on their authority to the bishops of the early church who in turn passed it on to the next generation. This doctrine affirms that apostolic authority today is found only in the bishops who are in direct succession from the original laying on of hands back unto the Apostles. This doctrine is held by Catholic, Eastern Orthodox, and Anglican churches.

[33] The "39 Articles" is the basic confession of faith for the Anglican Church (Episcopal in America). This is a very fine document.

CHAPTER SEVEN
THE PURITAN MOVEMENT

THE PURITAN MOVEMENT

As I study history I realize that the process of restoration is not a neat and simple progression. Many who believe in the restoration of the church do not realize how much truth was understood in earlier periods of history. This becomes clear in a study of the Puritan Movement. **The Puritan Movement was one of the most extraordinary movements in the history of the church.** Puritans had a great knowledge of Scripture and some of their writings read as though they were written yesterday (when put into modern language). One example is William Gurnell's *The Christian in Complete Armour*. Gurnell eventually became an Anglican, but his theology was Puritan. It was written in the mid 1600's and is amazingly relevant for today.

Some Puritans experienced extraordinary visitations of the Holy Spirit and entered into amazing depths of prayer, revival, and Holy Spirit manifestations. You can read about some of these visitations. Some recorded, "Ten men fell down during our prayer meeting last night, and they remained as dead all night long." They did not fully understand it. They continued, "We carried them out of the meeting, and the next day they told of dreams and visions of wonderful things that they had seen in the heavenlies." These were the kind of things that were going on in Puritan prayer meetings. **Many are unaware of this.**[34]

Some among the Puritans were the first to clearly record a belief in the restoration of Israel. Not all of the Puritans saw it. They were Reformed and Calvinistic. However, they maintained an amazingly positive heart towards the Jewish people. They saw themselves in the light of Jewish roots. The Puritans who came from England to America understood themselves as living out deliverance and a role parallel to the role of Israel. Their colonies were seen as a new Israel. In the thinking of many Puritans this was not replacement theology. The Puritans wanted to be a nation in the midst of nations that would be a light to the nations as Israel was meant to be. The phrase "city on a hill," a Puritan ideal (John Winthrop) that Ronald Reagan was fond of and quoted, needs to be understood in its Puritan meaning. They truly wanted to be a New Covenant Biblical society.

The Puritans of England actually replaced the monarchy and took over the government of England! It was sad that under the protectorate of Oliver Cromwell, Puritanism in England declined. When believers gain political leadership, there should be a better government. It is a remarkable thing to realize that the Puritans did rule England for a time and founded a nation!

Another contribution of the Puritans was their belief that the Law of God was to inform society - indeed that society had to come into conformity with the rule of God. They progressed toward democracy due to their understanding of a plurality of elders and the priesthood of believers. Elders were elected and accountable to an educated adult membership of a local congregation. This led them to democratic governmental directions.

The Puritans, however, did not rightly distinguish civil and religious government in the colonies. The Puritans depended upon the civil government to enforce church doctrinal fidelity. Roger Williams was closer to the truth of distinguishing civil and church government. The democracy of the United States was partially rooted in the writings of the Puritans. The church government of the Calvinists was the predecessor of the American Revolution and political freedom. The British called the American Revolution the "Presbyterian Revolution." It is amazing that we don't study these things in our schools. These are documented truths known by historians.

Some of the Puritans saw that one role of the church was to make Israel jealous and felt that the church's history with regards to the Jewish people was terrible. The Puritans invited the Jews from all over Europe to come to England and to the Colonies for refuge. The United States policy of favoring the Jewish people comes from the Puritan insight of revelation concerning Israel. We think of Reformed theology as being replacement theology, but this was not so among many of the Puritans. Samuel Rutherford, the author of Lex Rex[35], wrote the most poignant words of love concerning the heart attitude of Yeshua toward the Jewish people: "When they find each other again," he wrote, "how they would weep together!"

Therefore, the Puritans believed that in being a new Israel and a city set on a hill they had to show compassion to old Israel. Some of them even believed that the Jewish people needed to be restored to the land of Israel. It was a minority, but most of them began to believe that they had a role of showing compassion to Israel, opposing anti-Semitism, and making Israel jealous or desirous of faith in Yeshua (Romans 11). Increase Mather, in the Colonies, wrote a book on Romans 9-11 and the restoration of national Israel.[36]

The writings of the Puritans influenced Bishop Joseph Butler, who was an Anglican. In 1732 he wrote that we can expect that all of the promises to the Jewish people will be fulfilled, even the return to their land. You can read this in his apologetic, *The Analogy of Religion*, which for 150 years was the basic textbook of apologetics in English speaking seminaries and schools.

Unfortunately, Puritan influence and power in England declined and the monarchy came back. It was an anti-Puritan monarchy with Catholic leanings. Even in that darkness, the Puritans came to believe much of what I believe, even in the restoration of the church to unity and righteousness. **The Puritans will always be remembered for their courage, their fervency, their zeal for revival, and their call to holiness.**

Did they understand all God's healing promises, the gifts of the Holy Spirit, and all about five-fold ministry? No. Some were a-millennial; some were post-millennial; some didn't define the millennial issue clearly. Some were so unclear that it is hard to know exactly where they stood. They did believe that the succession of revivals would issue in a great world harvest before the coming of the Lord. In that last great world harvest the church would come to a place of glory where Israel would be made jealous and be restored and re-engrafted. They believed this in the 1600's! Some believed in the restoration of the church and Israel together.

I want to encourage you to read a book that doesn't see Israel quite like we do in terms of the literal restoration. It is Ian Murray's, *The Puritan Hope*. It is an extraordinary book. Dr. Michael Brown in his book on anti-Semitism, *Our Hands are Stained with Blood*, quotes from the chapter on Christians and churches that treated Jewish people well. Thank God there were some. There were times in Israel's History where the Jews were faithful - the reign of David and the early years of Solomon. This is true of Church History as well. I say this for Jewish folks to not lose hope.

The Baptists in England were an off shoot of the Puritan Movement. They were Puritan in doctrine and Puritan in their government, at least in the beginning. The Colonial Puritans were not Presbyterian in government but had a more democratic orientation. In England, the Presbyterian Movement eventually predominated among Puritans. A little later in America, this was true also. Congregationalists lost their evangelical doctrines and some became Unitarians. Baptists came to believe that the Calvinist baptism doctrine was wrong and that there needed to be baptism by immersion only for adults (or at least those of the age of accountability who could make a true decision for Yeshua). This was the origin of the Baptist church as we know it - a powerful world-wide movement. Baptists eventually became more democratic with the pastor as elder and the board as deacons.

God gave the Church a tremendous gift when He gave her the Puritan Movement. The spiritual vitality, purity, zeal, and proper understanding of the Church and her role to Israel all served to help realign the Church much more closely to the Biblical standard of restoration truth. We would gain much benefit to our lives, individually and corporately, if we would study and apply many of the things the Puritans believed and did.

---

34 Puritans are often considered stodgy. It is commonly thought that they sat on hard chairs and pews to demonstrate discipline. Ushers did tickle congregants with a feather to wake them up if they fell asleep during the sermon, but the sermons were not neccessarily dry or boring even though they were often two hours long. Maybe some Puritans were like the stereotype, but the use of the word "Puritan" in our society having a negative meaning is certainly unwarranted.

35 *Law is King*, by Samuel rutherford, was a great treatise on government being accountable to law as it put forth democratic direction.

36 It is false to teach that the belief in a destiny for the Jewish people was the creation of J.N. Darby and his Dispensationalist followers in the nineteenth and twentieth centuries.

CHAPTER EIGHT
THE METHODIST MOVEMENT

THE METHODIST MOVEMENT

The Puritan Movement declined at the end of the 17th and the beginning of the 18th century. The fervor of the Spirit was lost. **Like many movements, it became an intellectual system that people merely affirmed.**[37] The next movement of restoration was the Methodist restoration.

The Methodist restoration was one of the greatest in history. It was led by two great apostolic figures, George Whitfield, the Calvinist, and John Wesley, the Armenian. The Methodists saw a **restoration of the Spirit** in their great evangelistic campaigns. They also **restored the method of discipleship through small group ministry** from which Methodism gets its name. Some things that we believe were only restored recently were actually present years before. During the days of John Wesley, the Methodists were Anglicans. They did not desire to leave the mother church in England. Most classical denominations were formed because people were not allowed to practice the truth they discovered in Scripture. They were forced to leave, though they were saddened by it. This was true of Lutheran, Reformed, Anabaptist, Methodist, and others. Today there are thousands of denominations and streams, and it is almost considered a good thing to start your own work. In the past, people thought it a grievous thing to divide. Schism was to be avoided if possible. To many in America it is a badge of honor to set up your shingle and start your own thing, whether as an independent congregation or a denomination. The early Methodists did not want to do this.

What did Methodism believe? **Wesley saw the need for people to have a personal conversion experience and to encounter the Holy Spirit.** In this he reaffirmed some of the Puritan emphasis. Wesley also believed in the method of small group discipleship and accountability. In the small group they would ask each other, "How goes it with your spiritual life. How is your devotional life, victory over sin, and your evangelistic witness?" Men would be raised up and discipled. Out of that discipling, people were sent out to preach the Gospel. It was basically what we call today the cell group structure.

Wesley never wanted to leave the Anglicans. He was raising up lay pastors and leaders and this was looked at negatively by the Anglican hierarchy which only wanted the ordained clergy to do the work of preaching the Gospel. After Wesley's death, Methodists were forced out. The Methodists still kept a hierarchy in government more like Anglicanism with regard to their ordained bishops, however, they still kept a small group orientation. **When they came to the United States, the Methodists became the most important revival movement of the nineteenth century.**

Combined with the moving of the Spirit, the small group method raised up countless church planters. This is why in most towns and hamlets there is a Methodist church. If you go to a little town and ask as you are driving down the road, "There's a little white church down there, what kind of church is it?" You can give ten to one odds that it's going to be a Methodist church. Why? The method and the Spirit.

Today the Methodist church has largely apostatized. Wesley would be so sad. The onslaught of evolutionism and secular humanism in the nineteenth century swept the Methodist seminaries at the turn of the century. Before this, the Methodists were winning converts. There were camp meetings, revival meetings, street preaching, teaching sessions, small groups, Methodist camps at the seashore, and Methodist camps in the woods! The Presbyterians, the people of the previous restoration, were offended. The earlier restoration tends to look down on the new restoration. It was said of the lay preachers, "They're not educated. They haven't a seminary degree."

Charles Finney originally was a Presbyterian. Finney defended the Methodists. "While we're looking down at these Methodists for their lack of education, they're doing the work! They are winning the world." Their small group discipleship method was the greatest evangelistic force in 19th century America. **The Methodist Movement was really a restoration of both the Spirit and the Biblical pattern of small groups and accountability.**

In the study of the Methodist Movement we can find the truth that when foundations and structures are Biblical - the release of God's Spirit and power is more greatly increased.

CHAPTER NINE
THE BEGINNINGS OF CHRISTIAN ZIONISM

THE BEGINNINGS OF CHRISTIAN ZIONISM: THE ANGLICAN-LUTHERAN MOVE TOWARD UNITY AND TOWARD ISRAEL

In the nineteenth century Frederick the Great of Prussia was studying the Word of God. There were truly spiritual people around him. Some, I believe, were influenced by the Moravians and Lutheran Pietists. When there is a real revival, often there is a concern for Israel. **Frederick believed, on the basis of John 17, that the Evangelical church needed to unite and become one.** He came to believe, on the basis of such unity, that they needed to establish a saved remnant of Israel in the land of Israel before they would see the glory of God and the return of Jesus. The King of Prussia came to believe this! He questioned how this could be done.

He had a leading Lutheran contact the archbishop of Canterbury of the Anglican church to convey to him that all evangelical believers needed to unite and to have a mission to Israel to express this unity. He offered to submit to the Anglicans in the organization of this mission. The Anglicans had both Lutheran and Reformed roots, because of this they had the opportunity to be a force for unifying leadership of both these roots. They believed their theology was close enough. The Lutherans argued that they needed to have a mission to Israel, to establish a

Protestant presence in the land of Israel so that there would be a saved remnant of Israel. There must be, they thought, a Jewish Christian presence in the land before Jesus comes back.

The Prussian theologians dialogued with the Anglican theologians and together they became convinced of what they needed to do. They went to Queen Victoria, the head of the Anglican church, and she too became convinced. In England, because church and state are not separated as in America, they went to the Parliament. The Parliament passed the Israel Mission as legislation in the 1840's! They didn't understand Messianic Jewish expression as we now do, but they planned something with similar features. They decided to try to find a Jew whom they could train to become the Protestant bishop in Jerusalem. This, they believed, would begin a Jerusalem movement of the saved remnant of Israel. They also wanted to encourage Jewish people to go back to the land of Israel. They saw themselves as players in fulfilling Biblical prophecy by their own conscious endeavors.

God does His work through His instruments. We can see here the beginnings of Christian Zionism. **If it were it not for Christian Zionists there would probably be no Jewish state today.** The plan was carried out and Bishop Alexander was appointed to Jerusalem. Norwegian Lutherans were also convinced and put up considerable funds for the work. Ultimately the plans were thwarted by the non-Protestant groups in the land. Palestine was ruled by Turkey, and the Orthodox and Catholics expected Turkey to keep the Protestants out. This became an international affair. Archbishop Alexander died a few years later. However, an Anglican church called Christ Church still survives inside the Joppa gate, which is the church that was then planted. Due to the political pressures the bishopric did not continue, but the church did. Today a Messianic Jewish congregation meets in that building!

The Jewish community does not see the great importance that Christian Zionists played in the existence of the state of Israel. The theology we spoke of was instrumental in bringing many key people into support for Israel. In the 19th century the Earl of Shaftsbury became prominent in Christian Zionist endeavors. British Major John Windgate is credited with training the Hagganah, the defense force for the Jewish people in Palestine before Israel became a state and later became the Israel Defense Force after the creation of the State of Israel. Wingate trained the Jewish forces to defend themselves against the onslaught of the Arab forces in the 1930's. The Balfour Declaration declared Palestine to be the homeland for the Jewish people before Palestine was under the British League of Nations mandate. Later, Great Britain went back on this declaration and was judged. Who was Arthur John Balfour who wrote the declaration named after him? He was the British Foreign Secretary **and** a Christian Zionist. Who is one of the men in the U. S. who greatly encouraged Theodore Hertzl, the father of the Jewish State? It was W. E. Blackstone, **another** Christian Zionist. Blackstone, who was a Christian missionary to the Jews in Chicago, founded the American Messianic Fellowship.

The workings of God are wonderful. Every prayer and every seed sown that was of God will be added up; the total force of it will be a key to save Israel in the last days. The prayers of all the Christians from history are adding up. There will be a generation that will see the triumph of the Kingdom of God. The promise of Romans 11 will take place.

CHAPTER **TEN**
RESTORATION MOVEMENTS
IN THE UNITED STATES

RESTORATION MOVEMENTS IN THE UNITED STATES
(NINETEENTH AND TWENTIETH CENTURY)

Because the churches of Europe were state churches, we do not find the same multiplication of denominations in countries outside of the United States as we have found inside the United States. The separation of civil and religious governments gave an opportunity of unparalleled freedom. A separation of civil government from responsibility to God was never intended – such a separation would be false doctrine. Unfortunately, many Jewish people think that they are safest in a secular state. I believe a secular state will ultimately turn on Jewish people because there is insufficient value commitment to maintain true compassion for others. Only a Biblically minded people provide safe haven for Jews. There is in our faith the foundation of a moral fiber to not fall into persecuting any man that is made in the image of God.

The concept of restoration became very prominent in the nineteenth century. Some saw the restoration of the church as a last-days priority. People spoke of creating or restoring true New Testament churches. These movements were trying to get back to a greater purity of New Testament church government, New Testament holiness, and New Testament empowerment. In these movements there were visitations of the Spirit. Because of their doctrine and convictions of Biblical government, some had to leave the structures or denominations they were in.

Most denominations in the nineteenth century came into existence because a group of people came to deep convictions on particular issues. Accordingly, they were not allowed to practice their convictions in the structures that existed. They had to go outside the camp to practice restoration truth. I want you to see this. In the seventeenth century the Baptists had to go outside the camp of the other Puritans. So it was in the nineteenth century when different people began to see what they perceived to be restoration truths. Sometimes their views were right and sometimes not right. Free churches in Europe believed in freedom from state control.

THE SEVENTH DAY MOVEMENT

The Seventh Day Movement reflected the conviction that restoration required the church to keep the seventh day Sabbath.[38] The Seventh Day people believed that they were restoring New Testament Christianity by worshipping on the seventh day. The Adventists were one group of Seventh Day people. Ellen White, who claimed to be a prophetess, was their leader. She claimed to receive a revelation that the Lord would return in 1848, but of course this didn't come to pass. She then claimed that He did partially return to the court of the tabernacle in heaven for an investigative judgment, but not yet to the earth. The Seventh Day Adventists saw a high place for the law and even obeyed the Biblical food laws. It is strange to me that the Sabbath became so important, yet the other feasts weren't emphasized. This was partly due to the Sabbath command being included in the Ten Commandments.

The Adventists saw themselves as the new Israel; they did not see a role for natural Israel. Adventists also believed that worship on Sunday was a mark of the beast, the anti-Christ. This produced a separation from other Christians. Some theologians question if Adventist doctrine is clear on salvation by grace. Other people in the Seventh Day Movement did not take such extreme positions. Seventh Day Baptists would be one example.

THE CHURCH OF GOD AND CHURCH OF CHRIST MOVEMENTS

Other movements of restoration included the Church of God (Anderson, Indiana), the Church of Christ (known for acapelo singing without musical instruments), and the Disciples of Christ. Many were reading the Word and seeking restoration, but coming to different conclusions. The Nazarenes and the Christian and Missionary Alliance were formed to be closer to New Testament truth. By the end of the nineteenth century there was hardly a combination of convictions that were not represented in some existent group. There was a multiplication of denominations.

THE HOLINESS MOVEMENT

The Holiness Movement was also a great movement of restoration which began to see a place of importance for Israel. There was a commitment to revival and world missions. The Holiness Movement was known for their camp meetings and successful missionary endeavors. Did it become legalistic? Yes. There was also great sincerity and piety. You can read some of the Holiness authors such as A. B. Simpson and A.J. Gordon who touched the lives of many people. They founded Nyack College and Gordon College respectively. These were significant movements of the Holy Spirit under apostolic men. Others taught physical healing as part of the blessing of the New Covenant. A. B. Simpson wrote a book on healing and the Holy Spirit. He accepted the reality of the gifts of the Spirit. Andrew Murray, a South African Presbyterian, wrote a book on healing as well. A. J. Gordon also taught on physical healing. Dispensationalists spoke well of these authors but did not distribute these books.[39] The Holiness Movement spawned the Nazerenes, the Christian Missionary Alliance, new Methodist groups, and impacted some of the old Methodist groups.

THE PENTECOSTAL MOVEMENT

At the end of the nineteenth century, while one part of the church was experiencing significant advance, many of the denominations began to apostatize as evolutionary ideas and humanistic orientations began to make major inroads into seminaries. This continues in the decline of the old denominations to this day. In the beginning of the 20th century the Pentecostal revival took place, which grew out of the soil of the Holiness Movement. This revival took place parallel to the early Zionist Movement and Hertzl's Zionist Congress. The Holiness Movement largely believed in gifts of the Holy Spirit, but was lacking in clarity of definition. The Pentecostal revival embraced the Second Blessing doctrine of the Holiness Movement and this was largely believed by Holiness, Wesleyans, and Alliance people.[40]

The Pentecostal Movement became a great movement. It did not begin with great numbers, but if you look at world missions you will see that the Pentecostal Movement is one of the greatest forces in world missions. We have to see that God is doing something through this movement. Non-pentecostals claimed that pentecostals were in heresy because they spoke in tongues. The pentecostals' response was to claim that other Christians do not have the baptism in Holy Spirit. Some on the other side even claimed that speaking in tongues was of the devil. The Nazarene denomination made speaking in tongues an offense for discipline. Holiness ranks were divided.

By the end of the second decade of the 20th century the pentecostals were organizing into associations. They formed denominations (some do not like to use this word) to further their movement. God was restoring something in the operation of the gifts and power of the Holy Spirit. The Assemblies of God were formed. Later, the Pentecostal Holiness denomination and the Church of God in Cleveland, Tennessee were formed. There were differences in government and practices among different Pentecostal groups. One heretical denomination also formed, the United Pentecostal. They believed that Jesus and the Father are the same person. When Jesus was praying to the Father, He was simply praying to His higher self. This group was looked down upon by the other Pentecostal churches.

The Apostolic Pentecostal Church, another denomination, which is strong in Australia, taught the restoration of five-fold ministry in government (apostles, prophets, evangelists, pastors, and teachers). Due to black and white divisions, the black community formed the Church of God in Christ, today the largest Pentecostal denomination in America.

THE DISPENSATIONAL MOVEMENT: A REPUDIATION OF THE IDEA OF THE RESTORATION OF THE LAST-DAYS CHURCH

A movement came about in the nineteenth century that was a restoration of some truths. It has both praiseworthy qualities and bad qualities. **This movement was the Plymouth Brethren Movement in**

England under John Darby, who gave the world Dispensational theology.[41] This theology has some strong points as well as some points in its classical form, that I disagree with. I have found that it is very hard today to find a classical dispensationalist. There is much revision. John Darby, who was a great influence on the Scoffield Reference Bible, saw deadness in the Anglican church. One of his emphases was that there should be an educated laity who would lead the church. It should be a plurality of elders. A "plurality of elders" is a watchword of Brethren theology. Darby taught that communion should be only for those who were righteous members of a Brethren group. These were called Closed Brethren. Those from other denominations could not participate. The Closed Brethren influenced Watchman Nee in his early years, but he could not abide their separatism. **The Brethren came to a very strong belief in the restoration of Israel.** The literal future millennium (pre-millennialism) is also a very strong and positive teaching of Dispensationalism. I believe this thrust is basically correct. **Dispensationalism defined the Millennial Age and the reality of Israel in the Millennial Age in the greatest clarity that had been seen since the Apostolic Age.**

On the other hand, within Dispensationalism there were certain ways of making distinctions that I am very troubled about. **Darby defined a doctrine of grace** (which is still taught by some today) **whereby a person can be saved without submitting to the Lordship of the King, Yeshua.** I believe that this was a radically different understanding of the Gospel. In Dispensationalism you can receive Jesus as Savior, but may or may not later receive Him as Lord. You can come to believe in Jesus but do not have to repent, otherwise they argue that this would be works.

When I was a youngster, I attended Word of Life camp in upstate New York under Jack Wyrtzen. This was a major discipling source in my life for which I am forever grateful. I can remember that they would preach salvation Saturday, Sunday, Monday, and Tuesday. The orientation was "What have you got to lose? Say the prayer and go to heaven." There is no life change required. After Tuesday the teaching changed. The emphasis was that you can continue to sin and not commit your life to the Lord and still go to heaven, but you'll be miserable if you don't commit. How can you do that in the light of the One who was crucified for you? Wednesday, Thursday, and Friday they would try to get everybody to commit their lives to the Lord. There were campfire dedication meetings. They perceived two different experiences: one **salvation**, and one **dedication**. Why? Because if you have to accept Jesus as Lord to be saved then grace is not grace. They understood grace as undeserved favor from God. However, they lost sight of the dimension of grace that is for the purpose of empowerment to enable one to believe God and submit to the rule of the King. Biblical grace carries the power of obedience. You can't receive grace if you are intending to live in sin. The Gospel is the good news of the undeserved invitation to come back into the Father's house under the rule of the Father and the King (Luke 15). **Grace is the empowerment to obey the Word.**

In Dispensationalism, language about salvation was changed. The nineteenth century evangelists spoke about the number of people that made professions of faith. Whether or not they were saved would be proven (in Calvinism) by whether or not they would bring forth fruit and make their calling and election sure. In Armenianism, the profession was proved as true by the holy life of fruitfulness. They never said that a person was saved in their meeting, but that a person made a profession of faith. By contrast, Dispensationalism would say that a person was saved at their meetings. According to this theology, one could be saved and never produce real fruit, and still go to heaven. Their doctrine of grace was such that simply praying "the prayer" was enough. You might never see the person again; they might never join in fellowship, but if they believed for salvation and said the sinners prayer, they were saved. Of course, not all dispensationalists believe this today. Some do.[42]

Dispensationalism taught that the supernatural gifts of the Spirit were not for this age but only for the period before Scripture was given. Despite this, the other features of Dispensationalism swept the Pentecostal Movement in the 1920s. Many Bible schools and Christian colleges also became Dispensational.

There were other distinctions as well. **The Old Testament era was considered a dispensation of Law contrasted with New Covenant as a dispensation of Grace.** Distinctions were made between Israel and the Church whereby if one was part of Israel, then such a one was part of the covenant of law which will be reestablished in the Millennial Age for Israel. If one was part of the Church, then such a one was part of the covenant of grace

My understanding is that both covenants are gracious covenants, but because grace without the Holy Spirit under the Mosaic Covenant was not adequate, God took more of the responsibility to fulfill the Covenant in us through the immersion in the Holy Spirit and the promise of writing the law upon our hearts. I am more Reformed with regard to law and grace, but I'm more Dispensational with regards to the role of Israel in the Millennial Age.

In Classical Dispensationalism, one has to keep Israel and the Church separate. Originally in Dispensationalism, it was considered very wrong for a Jewish believer to live a Jewish life because that was considered a confusion of the dispensations. At the turn of the century, when Zionism was in its early years, a movement began that was called the Messianic Jewish Movement. There was a journal called *The Messianic Jew*, by Theodore Luckey and another journal called *The Hope of Israel*, edited by A. C. Gabelein and G. Stroker. These last two men started a mission in New York. In that mission, Gabelein once preached in Yiddish to 1,000 orthodox Jews at the turn of the century. Gabelein was calling for the formation of Messianic congregations. There was such a move in Europe led by Lukey, an Adventist.[43]

Then Gabelein read Dispensational theology and became convinced that he had been wrong. He became convinced of classic Dispensational distinctions. Therefore, the idea of the saved remnant of Israel, in the sense of Jews living a Jewish life in the New Covenant, was nullified. It was wrong to be both a Christian and a Jew, both part of the Bride and the earthly Israel. He came to believe that if one is born a Jew and has become a believer in Yeshua and is still living as part of the destiny of Israel, or is living a Jewish life, then such a one has confused the dispensations. One is either part of the Bride, and the one new man (where there's neither Jew nor Gentile), or one is part of Israel. Dispensational theology claimed that no person could be part of both by this distinction. So Gabelein gave up his mission in New York and became a famous Dispensational theologian; indeed, he became one of the key editors of the Scofield Reference Bible that summarized Dispensational teaching. His partner did not agree with Dispensational distinctions. Infact, he so passionately disagreed that he went back to Germany to continue the work.

Those that were influenced by Classical

Dispensationalism in Jewish missions sometimes produced Hebrew Christian churches. If they were classical dispensationalists, they didn't keep a Passover Seder, but only perhaps an art picture on the wall of a Seder table. Some would have a Passover demonstration, because it was considered wrong to actually have a Passover Seder. I believe that the relationship between the covenants was mistaught. This movement presented its teaching with great clarity and power so that some of its weaknesses were overlooked. The movement swept the churches and Bible schools in America, even the Pentecostal schools, though it taught that the gifts of the Holy Spirit were only for a transitional dispensation before the New Testament Scripture was written.

In my view, the Dispensational brethren restored some aspects of new Testament government and doctrine. However, they lost the Puritan hope of the true Church being restored to power, holiness, and the unity Christ prayed for in John 17. They were pessimistic about the last-days Church, which they believed would be raptured out before the Tribulation, thus significant restoration of the Body was not emphasized. In the 20th century, waiting for an any-minute rapture became the focus. The Puritan idea of our Christian lifestyle influencing our vocation and influencing all of culture was lost. The prevailing thought was, "Why save a sinking ship?" The view that Kingdom living and witness brought us closer to His return was also lost.

THE THEOLOGY OF GEORGE LADD : His impact on my Life

My spiritual father, who was the dearest and most saintly man I have ever known, was the late Chaplain Evan Welsh of Wheaton College. He nursed Patty and me back to faith through our own times of personal crisis. He was both a Presbyterian and a 19th century holiness person all at the same time. He was a person of great godliness who was continually manifesting the presence of God. His father was the pastor of College Church in Wheaton (not affiliated with Wheaton College). It was called College Church because it was right across the street from the campus. College Church became divided over Dispensational theology. Previously they taught a classical Holiness theology. The church split and Chaplain Welsh's father lost his pulpit. Through this and other tragedies his father lost his mind. It was a real anguish to Chaplain Welsh but he grew in compassion because of the depth to which he responded to tragedy with godliness. He knew much tragedy - his first wife died when their three daughters were young. He had a great capacity to love.

Evan Welsh went to Princeton Seminary and became convinced of the pre-millennial view as well as a place for Israel. After Seminary, Evan pastored College Church. Then he pastored Ward Memorial Presbyterian Church in Detroit. After pastoring at Ward, he became the chaplain at Wheaton College, and during his later years there he became the interim pastor of Adat Ha Tikvah in Chicago, back when it was still called the First Hebrew Christian Church. He was often called upon by the Presbytery to put salve on the pain of splits and to resolve difficult situations. Because I was a favored person whom he had helped, he imposed upon me to become the student pastor of this Hebrew Christian Church twenty-three years ago when I was still in seminary. This was a key reason why I came into the Messianic Jewish Movement. Evan Welsh impacted every area of our lives and was the model by which we now understand spirituality. His impact on my wife, Patty, and me was so incredible that it is hard to comprehend.[44]

In terms of eschatology, I was trained at Word of Life, and then discipled in the Reformed church in

Replacement theology. I can remember sitting in his living room. I was a new seminary student. On that day as I was studying the book of Revelation, I said to myself, "It's hopeless. Nobody can ever figure this stuff out." I thought, "Maybe eschatology is just conditional. If we're really good and succeed in evangelism, the terrible events of the book of Revelation won't happen. If we're really bad it will all come!" Sometimes I thought, partly jesting to myself, maybe if we believe, we'll get out at the beginning of the seven year tribulation, and if we don't we'll get out at the mid-tribulation point, or after the tribulation." Basically, I was skeptical about the last of the last-days. I thought that people who taught detailed last-days eschatology were ignorant and did not realize all of the possibilities or how difficult it was to know the truth of these things. I tried to bypass it. I did not understand that in a significant sense that New Testament theology is eschatology. The Kingdom has broken in. You can't bypass it. I didn't understand this as a young seminary student at Trinity in Chicago.

Once when I was visiting Chaplain Welsh he started talking about a book he had just finished reading by George Ladd called *The Gospel of the Kingdom, Essays on the Kingdom of God in New Testament Theology*. He gave me this book and with tears in his eyes he said to me, "The theology that my father preached is being restored to the church. I want you to read this book." I was quite touched when he gave me this book with such emotion.

I read the book and was amazed. I understood for the first time the views I now regularly teach regarding the Kingdom of God having already come and regarding the nature of the Gospel of the Kingdom. What I put forth is basically the George Ladd view on this. It is my revision of it, but is basically in accord with what I discovered 24 years ago:

the Kingdom has truly come where the Spirit has been given, but will not come in fullness until His return.

How do I look at the Dispensationalist Movement? Well there is good and bad; tremendous good and serious problems. I have Reformed dimensions and Dispensational dimensions in my thought. As I talk to Dispensationalist leaders, I find that many are re-thinking theologies. I think it's all part of God's work to get us all to re-think and to bring us together.

THE LATTER RAIN MOVEMENT

Pentecostalism continued to grow and is still alive and growing even in our own day. In the late 1940's there was an out-pouring of the Spirit in Canada which led to a movement of the Spirit that became very controversial. It was called the Latter Rain Movement. **The Latter Rain Movement was a movement of people being filled with the Holy Spirit and being restored to the gift of prophecy.**

There was a minor off-shoot of the Latter Rain Movement in 1948 called the Manifest Sons Movement. This heresy taught that the Body of Believers was going to be translated and glorified on earth before the return of the Lord. They would witness as manifest sons. Some gave up the work of evangelism to wait for their perfection.[45] This movement began to isolate itself and unfortunately, came to be identified with this minor off-shoot.

The Kingdom Now Movement[46] is being misrepresented as Replacement in theology. This is inaccurate. The Kingdom Now Movement is a movement of charismatics who discovered Reformed theology. That's all it is! Because Reformed theology had significant Replacement proponents, some Kingdom Now people are Replacement. Most are a-millennial, some are post-millennial, some are premillennial. Just because somebody says that something is off in a movement, some come to believe that the whole movement must be totally bad! There's good and bad in all Evangelical movements. I have tried to influence the Kingdom Now proponents toward the Puritans and seeing the place of Israel in the last days. Because I have a Reformed background I can speak into this situation with some empathy.

The Latter Rain Movement emphasized prophecy. It also taught the place of five-fold ministry for today (apostles, prophets, evangelists, pastors, and teachers). They emphasized the importance of ministry with the laying on of hands.

Those who teach the parallel restoration of the Church and Israel point out the timing parallels of late nineteenth century revivalism and early Zionism, the early Pentecostal revivals and the movement of Hertzl, and the Latter Rain Movement with the healing revivals of the late 1940's and the early 1950's and the independence of the state of Israel.[47] People began to wonder if there is an intention of God whereby spiritual visitations in the Church take place during the same period of significant steps forward in Israel's modern history? The Latter Rain Movement had world-wide influence. Pentecostals were divided over it and the classical denominations did not as a whole accept it.

THE CHARISMATIC MOVEMENT

In the late 1960's the Charismatic Movement came to full bloom. Amazingly, this world-wide movement took place at the same time God was restoring something in Israel. This time the parallel was to the Six Day War and the Old City part of Jerusalem coming into Israeli governmental control. Some people say Jerusalem is still trodden down because the Gentiles (the Moslem temple) occupy the temple mount. This is only by Israeli deference.

Nineteen sixty-seven was a watershed time in the Charismatic Movement. In my senior year of high school (December 1964), I received a significant filling of the Holy Spirit through leaders in the Dutch Reformed church that I was a part of. They had been connected to the Charismatic Movement. I didn't speak in tongues until some years later. That might upset some people's theology, but I received such a filling! I was totally strange for three weeks. I couldn't sing a hymn without tears. I was in a secular high school where very few were believers! It was very secular and was one of the top academic high schools in New Jersey. Prior to this experience I had always tried to be a witness, and struggled to win classmates to the Lord. After this experience, I walked through the halls and sat in my classes as if on a cloud. I was able to see several students come to profess faith that year.

This move of the Holy Spirit was holy. People were cleaning up their lives after experiencing the Spirit. They were committing themselves to Scriptural study. It was largely a movement in the context of the church, as in my case within the Dutch Reformed church. As so often happens, the establishment was fearful of new moves of the Spirit as they feared losing control. People began to find themselves ostracized, being given the left foot of disfellowship. On the other hand, some were divisive, impatient with other believers, and were judging people by whether or not they had the Holy Spirit on the basis of whether or not they spoke in tongues (or whether or not they had certain other experiences).[48]

Divisions came; many people in the Charismatic Movement believed that they could not live out their convictions within the structure of the existent churches. The saying that new wine can not be put in old wine-skins was a common refrain. People started leaving their churches and forming independent charismatic organizations and independent apostolic flows, which I call the new mini-denominations, under the oversight of an apostolic leader. He may or may not have believed in a plurality of other leaders to which he was accountable.[49] Yet, in the new charismatic separation groups there was no consensus on government, accountability, or ethics. Some claimed authority as God's anointed and they were not to be corrected by other humans. Others developed rigid structures. Some people in independent churches were so loose that anything was accepted under the view that we are not to judge others.

The Charismatic Movement spawned the Jesus Movement. It was a tremendous movement that swept many people into the Kingdom. However, the spirit of lawlessness from the anti-Vietnam war movement also came into the movement. Many of the charismatics that were saved were anti-organizational and lacked a true understanding of the Body of Believers. **Much of the Charismatic world became either anarchistic or authoritarian.**[50]

Charismatics, as seen on television and reported in various forms of media, have been open to every wind of doctrine. The independent charismatics adapted an entrepreneurial and entertainment orientation. Churches were in free enterprise competition for the people who believed in Yeshua. Denominations have always been competing. However, this intensified in the Charismatic world since loyalty to denominations and flows was at a low point and status was found in building a big church. You had Macy's, and you had Gimble's in New York. There was competition between the Baptists and the Presbyterians. However, in the new independent Charismatic churches, the orientation was to advertise (to the Christian public), "Come to our church.

We will love you more, make you happier, give you more for your tithe."[51]

The classical Evangelicals required more in basic moral standards for members and leaders than did most of the Charismatic churches. I do believe that there was a loss of understanding Church government and standards which was once restored in the Reformation under Calvin. **Some charismatics believed in five-fold ministry, but failed to see that five-fold ministers should be held to the standard of elders or at least deacons in character attainment.** Furthermore, there was also a loss of understanding that elders were to enforce God's standards in the church and to see that loving and legitimate discipline is part of congregational life. In anarchy there was a repudiation of the denominational roots of the church. Pride prevents one from learning from Church History's wisdom and mistakes.

There was a plethora of groups, a multiplication of independent congregations and flows. Awesome fragmentation took place. Anybody who said they had a calling, without anybody to endorse them as elders in character and to hold them in Biblical accountability, could go out and set up a sign as a leader. If they had good hype, and if they had good charisma, they gathered a group. Unfortunately, many of these "leaders" did not know how to disciple and care for people, and as a result a tremendous moral decline in the American church was produced. Such has to be reversed. I believe that true elders must ordain true elders and that this pattern can be traced all the way back to the Apostles. I do not believe in self-appointment though one may have a calling from God.

DISCIPLESHIP MOVEMENT

Many charismatics who saw these trends were glad

to stay within their classical denominations or to join classical Pentecostal associations. **In seeing these problems, a group of men formed the Discipleship, Shepherding Movement.** They saw a great need for order, standards, and government. They saw the anarchy. Some in this movement swung all the way to a control orientation and required that all personal decisions in a member's life be approved by their shepherd. A national hierarchy was formed. To avoid being anarchistic these men swung all the way to the other place and begin to supersede the conscience of the individual believer. There was an accountability hierarchy such that each level of leadership was accountable to a higher level until it reached the plurality of the top five leaders. It was an Episcopal denominational structure with five leaders at the top. This movement produced a great reaction in other charismatics. In our humanity and sin we swing to extremes. Today the Discipleship Movement is fragmented and many of the original leaders have repented. However, the problems they sought to address are still with us.

THE WORD OF FAITH MOVEMENT

The father of the Word of Faith Movement was Kenneth Hagin of Rhema Bible School in Tulsa, Oklahoma. Thousands of ministers and churches around the world today still identify with this movement. It is a movement rooted in both classical Pentecostalism and the Charismatic Movement. What is restored here? It is a reemphasis of early Pentecostal beliefs reflected in such writers as John Lake, F. F. Bosworth, Smith Wigglesworth, and Stanley Frodshezim. This movement restored the view that the promises of God are to be believed and received through the study of, meditation on, and confession of the Word of God. God really meant what He said when He gave these promises. There are many teachers of varied doctrinal solidity in this movement.[52] Does the Word of Faith Movement have a good understanding of church government? No. They teach a royal pastor headship. However, a recent book by Kenneth Hagin taught that ministers should be accountable in a ministerial association. Some leaders in this movement have taught a wrong doctrine of prosperity, defending ministers living in sumptuous opulence. This is never a good testimony. Yet there is a promise of abundant provision for those who are generous. Do they have good understanding of other doctrines? The record is quite mixed. William Artega in *Quenching the Spirit* has a good evaluation. I believe that there is something that God is restoring about faith being built into our lives through the Word and the certainty of His promises. The Word of Faith Movement has brought this emphasis to the fore.

THE VINEYARD MOVEMENT

John Wimber, the head of the Vineyard, has had a profound effect in the American church world. **Combining the theology of George Ladd as a foundation of understanding the Kingdom, and the role of signs and wonders as manifestations of the Kingdom, Wimber has influenced countless evangelicals to embrace the gifts and power of the Holy Spirit. The Vineyard is trying to combine a seriousness of Evangelical doctrine with Charismatic experience.** This movement does not endorse tongues as the essential sign of the baptism of the Spirit. This has produced significant openings. Scholarship is combined with spiritual power. The one great weakness I see in the Vineyard is a lack of clarity in membership standards for people. If you participate then you are a member. If you don't, you are not. The classical commitment to membership standards is crucial in establishing a real membership covenant and in being able to enforce church discipline. American courts allow for church discipline only if there is a clear membership covenant. However, the Vineyard Movement has been progressing toward clear leadership standards. Leading Evangelical scholars have written in support of the Vineyard Movement (Wayne Grudem of Trinity, Peter Wagner of Fuller, and John White).

In the nineteenth and twentieth centuries much restoration of Biblical truth had transpired in the United States. In just two hundred years, key restoration truths had been restored to the Church and have since radically transformed the face of the Church into what we now know it as. May we continue to learn how to lay hold of the good, reject the bad, and push on to the better!

38 My own understanding of this is that there is an accommodation in this transitional age to not require the Sabbath for all Christians. However, there is no Sabbath replacement by Sunday either. In the Age to Come the whole world will be seventh day oriented.

39 We are all dispensationalists to some degree if we do not believe we are under Mosaic order. However, the question is how we draw the boundaries or define dispensations. We're all Reformed too! We are reformed and are reforming!

40 The "Second Blessing" refers to the baptism of the Holy Spirit, however, Pentacostalism taught that one did not have this experience unless one spoke in tongues. I believe in speaking in tongues but one cannot prove that this is necessary for proving baptism in the Holy Spirit. Both Moody and Torrey believed in the baptism of the Holy Spirit. They were part of the Holiness Movement. I do believe that those baptized in the Spirit can speak in tongues, but it does not necessarily follow that one does not have the baptism without speaking in tongues.

41 Dispensationalist theology is a scheme of Biblical interpretation that divides history into several distinct eras or "dispensations." Though according to Scofield there are seven dispensations, generally Dispensationalism is understood as suggesting three (OT dispensation of law, present dispensation of grace, and the future dispensation of the millennial Kingdom following the second advent of Christ.)

42 We become much more aware of the realities of language. When we

talk in such terms, saying that a person was saved at a meeting, do you recognize the implications of this phrasing? **Language either reveals reality or conceals reality.** Language is important. We should note that dispensationalists did require a standard of holiness for church membership and emphasized holy living. They truly wanted people to dedicate their lives to the Lord and receive the life of joyful service available to them.

43 Yes, there was a Messianic Jewish Movement in the early days of Zionism.

44 You would have to have known the man to understand how impacting his life was. Thousands of people who knew him and who came to his funeral had some understanding of it.

45 I believe we are to show that we are children of God, but not in this sense. We should be filled with the Spirit and be holy. However, the full manifestation of glorified bodies does not take place until the return of the Lord.

46 Kingdom Now theology believes that the Kingdom of God should be showing itself now. This belief affirms that Biblical principles should be manifesting themselves in every realm of life.

47 God did judge the Healing Movement, which was a part of the Latter rain Movement, when leaders fell into sins of greed and immorality and it declined.

48 I do believe there is a filling in the Spirit and if you've had it, you know it. I believe that a person can be filled with the Holy Spirit many times. The initial time you have that experience it changes your life and it is distinct. from then on you can walk in the Spirit.

49 I believe that if you ever teach that a leader is beyond accountability so that they cannot be removed for sin, you are in serious error!

50 Teaching non-accountability or the royal-pastor model is a serious error. A church without standards for leaders and members is in danger of going into heresy. On the other hand, a church that supersedes conscience and the leading of the Holy Spirit and the Word (to follow leadership instead of the leading of the Holy Spirit) is also heresy.

51 It is amazing how much church advertising on radio and television is toward the believer, not to the lost!

52 We also have to understand that we are in a partial stage of Kingdom manifestation so one never attains promises perfectly in this life.

CHAPTER ELEVEN
CONCLUSION

CONCLUSION

Where are we now in the Charismatic world? First, there is still the Charismatic contingent in the older denominations which continues to be significant. Second, we see independent churches of all sizes. We see the "Cell Church" emphasis affecting many by the teaching of David Cho, Ralph Neighbor, Dale Galloway, Carl George, and others. We also continue to see the franchising orientation of apostolic flows. While we see the problems outlined above, sometimes God will use the problems and the decline to wake people up to what He wants. God is not in favor of competing denominations and flows which cause fragmentation of the Body. He is not calling for apostolic flows that are isolated from one another in each city and are loyal only to their flow or denomination. The franchised and independent say, "Come and buy my product because its better than the product of the church down the street." Whether it is the Assemblies of God, or the apostolic flow of a particular man, Word of Faith church, Evangelical, or other, we see this attitude: "Come to us, we have sound doctrine. Come here, you'll be healed. Come here, I'm more entertaining. Come here for what we've got in our children's program." The nature of church life at the end of the twentieth century is multiple denominations and apostolic flows without inter-accountability, prayer, or cooperative effort. There are some great exceptions. Thank God! The Christian public needs to be educated out of its Biblical naivete. Many churches start on radio to draw the Christian public. **In all of this we are not winning the lost.**[53] What have we gained from it all? The money that is spent in media for evangelism (there is a place for media) could be better spent on evangelism in the local church. Ninety percent of those who receive the Lord do so by the witness of a friend.

INDICATIONS OF HOPE

There are signs of hope. I believe it is God's intention to unify all true believers in the power of the Holy Spirit and to bring all the truths of all the restorations together in the end. What is happening to give hope?

First, is the hope of the Cell Church model. In Cell Churches, one does not go to church for the sake of only being served by the product offered. One becomes part of a community, accountable to a cell, and equipped to be effective in witness to lost people. Some mega-churches are great service centers, but do not build community. People who are built into community and who serve each other effectively do not easily switch to become part of another church. Biblically, membership in the church is not where one goes to hear good messages (this can be done by T. V. or tapes). It is where one is built into community, accountability, and is equipped to do the work of ministry. The elders and spouses are accountable to each other, they oversee cell leaders, and model what they teach. Cell congregations are more secure about their membership and tend to be more cooperative with other congregations in an area. The central meeting is a celebration, but the gifts of the Spirit, as in a I Corinthians 14 type meeting, are more operative in the smaller cell group setting. The cell meetings are considered more important than the central meetings. This is one of the great waves of the future Church. Successful cell leaders become overseers of cells. Overseers of cells become new missionaries and planters of congregations. In this model, Bible college can function in an adjunct capacity to this on-the-job training. This is a true Biblical restoration.

The second great indication of hope are new moves for unity among leaders and churches in various cities. David DuPlesis began to work toward this end. Such men as Francis Frangipane and John Dawson have powerfully made the case for coming together in integrity, love, prayer, and cooperative unity in every locality. I believe that God wants to gather us together in each city or locality and to break down the walls of competition and fear. We need to seek the heart of the Lord for unity cross-denominationally. This is happening in Cedar Rapids, Kansas City, California, Nashville, and in other cities in significant ways.

Such unity does not destroy ethnicity or a Jewish distinctive call. This was the great prayer of Yeshua and may be the last great stage in restoration. In the unity seen in John 17, the Church will be given a heart to overcome its competition and to join together in mutual accountability and cooperation across denominational and apostolic lines. This will include the acceptance of the power of the Holy Spirit that will break down the barriers. It will include moral and doctrinal foundations of stability. There will be mutual support in disciplinary situations. In the last-days revival our various apostolic flows and denominations will decrease in importance, and the Lord will raise up the Body in each city in greater importance. The church of the city will increase. As John the Baptist said, "He must increase and I must decrease." So also the Church seen in John 17 must increase and our competing flows and denominations and our lack of standards must decrease as God raises up a church in unity and accountability that has within it the truths of all of the past restoration movements.

Lastly, this church will also recover an appreciation of its Jewish roots of self understanding. It will make room for a Jewish expression in that city that is distinct as well as part of the larger church of the city. Jewish members of other churches will be encouraged to be Jewish for the enrichment of the church. There is an important place for encouraging the saved remnant of Israel. In recovering the unity of the church, the church will see that it has as its capstone victory the salvation of Israel. The church will see that by prayer and showing mercy they will help establish the saved remnant of Israel. In fact, they will see that this is part of their calling. This will lead to all Israel being saved.

World missions and making Israel jealous is the two-pronged mission of the whole Church in every age. I believe that the restoration of understanding Jewish roots is part of that coming to unity and is a key to transcending the many divisions that exist. Will we find unity in understanding more by Presbyterian, Baptist, or Pentecostal roots? No. Further progress will come from a more accurate Biblical contextual understanding of our Jewish roots!

It may look like we've become fragmented, carnal, and non-accountable. However, people will become disgusted with the situation and go on higher than the church has yet been. The Holy Spirit can open the eyes of leaders in the church all over the world. Thank God, "It is written." This is my hope.

53 According to recent statistics, we are seeing almost no net growth in numbers in North American Church. *Christianity Today* did a survey and they said that 95% of the people in the American mega-churches are from other churches rather than converts won by evangelism.

ONEPEOPLE MANY TRIBES

SUMMARY

SUMMARY

We have seen an amazing history of restoration since the Reformation. We have not noted that even the Catholic Church reformed as a result of these restorations. It has been two steps forward and one step back. We have seen faith and Scriptural authority restored by Luther. In the Reformed and Puritan movements, we see the restoration of Biblical church government. The Puritans had a special love for the Jewish people. The Reformed also brought the Biblical understanding of vocation and the cultural (creation) mandate to take dominion and to demonstrate the principles of the Kingdom or the Word over all realms of life. The Lutheran Pietists and Moravians emphasized prayer, holiness, and world missions. Some had a significant heart for Jewish people and their salvation. The Moravians prayed for 100 years at Havaline, birthing modern missions. In the Methodists, we saw small group accountability and sanctification restored to higher levels. Historic revivals were great leaps forward. The Anabaptists and Baptists restored immersion baptism for adults. The Holiness Movement (Finney, Moody, Murray, and Torrey) restored a deeper life walk. They began the Healing Movement at the end of the 19th century. The Pentecostal Movement restored greater clarity on the gifts of the Spirit and the use of the gift of tongues. The Latter Rain Movement restored the place of prophecy, the laying on of hands for spiritual gifts, and five-fold ministry. Earlier movements anticipated later restorations. In the 19th century there were many restoration movements.

Later restorations were amazingly parallel to God's work in restoring the nation of Israel. Early Zionism was parallel to the Holiness Movement. The movement of Hertz's Zionist Jewish Congress was parallel to the early Pentecostal Movement. The independence of Israel was parallel to the Latter Rain Movement and the Healing Revival of the late 1940's and early 1950's. The capture of the old city of Jerusalem in 1967 is parallel to the early Charismatic Movement and the Jesus Movement. This was the birth of the modern Messianic Jewish Movement too!

Today we look for a new revival and restoration. We see it in some other parts of the world more than in America. **It is a move of unity, prayer, holiness, and accountability in every locality.** It will be a concern for the success of every legitimate New Testament congregation. **It will be a move that recovers a Jewish rooted understanding of the church and affirms the legitimacy of the saved remnant of Israel.** This is not yet a majority in the church, but it is a growing minority.

I want to encourage you. There will be a restored Body of Believers in the last days that with its Jewish members will make Israel jealous. All Israel will be saved. Yeshua will return and deliver Israel and establish his world wide Kingdom. We will rule and reign with Him forever!

OTHER BOOKS
BY DR. JUSTER

DUE PROCESS
A plea for Biblical justice among God's people. "Must reading" for every leader in the body of Messiah – a challenge to function and govern biblically.

JEWISH ROOTS
A foundation of Biblical Theology. A significant book on Messianic Judaism which offers insight on many difficult questions.

GROWING TO MATURITY
A Messianic Jewish guide. This book is used by many congregations for membership classes.

These books are available through **Tikkun International Books**, P.O. Box 2997, Gaithersburg, MD 20886, Phone 301-977-0156, Fax 301-670-3820, E-mail tikmin@aol.com. To receive the Tikkun Newsletter and/or Tikkun catalog send in the coupon below by mail, fax, or e-mail us your details.

Name

Address

City/State/Zip

Phone   **Fax**   **E-mail**
Please send me :
☐ Latest Tikkun Newsletter   ☐ Latest Tikkun Catalog

TIKKUN INTERNATIONAL

PURPOSE

Tikkun is an international ministry dedicated to the restoration of Israel and the Church.

DESCRIPTION

Tikkun International is a network of congregations and ministry leaders that focuses on two primary objectives. The first is to be a sending agency for those called into Messianic Jewish ministry, both domestic and foreign.

The second is to join leaders, ministries, and congregations together into a network - building covenant relations, strengthening mutual support, and equipping leaders. These networks exist under a five-fold council of leadership called the Governing Council. In so doing, *Tikkun International* gives its leaders opportunities to give beyond their local congregations in serving and equipping the Body of Yeshua (both domestically and overseas).

The *Tikkun International* network provides a context for accountability and operates as a sending-agency support service. This is provided for those who share our distinct convictions and are drawn to be part of the network. *Tikkun* also maintains close relationships with Church networks of similar convictions that are supportive of our Messianic Jewish calling.

For more information on *Tikkun International* call our offices at 301-977-0156

{EAGLES' WINGS}

Impacting Destiny

"PREPARE THE WAY OF the Lord!" the prophet Isaiah cried out. Eagles' Wings is a relational network of believers from around the world who are striving to learn in our day and age what it really means to be a people who prepare the way of the Lord in our individual hearts, our churches, cities, and the nations of the world.

In all that we do - through our **nationwide conferences**, **international missions**, and **special events in Israel**, our **publishing of books, journals**, and **worship recordings**, and our **internship program** - we seek to become totally devoted followers of Jesus and lead others to life in Him.

Our mission is to be a catalyst for spiritual awakening and unity to people around the world.

We want to give you an opportunity to become more acquainted with us and find out how you can become a part of Eagles' Wings. There are many ways to be involved. We especially ask you to consider partnering with us by joining the Impact Destiny Team (IDT), those people who are linked with us in a vital way.

Prayerfully seek what the Lord would have you do, and then contact us. Just call the toll free number listed below. We are excited to invite you to join us.

PO BOX 450, CLARENCE, NY 14031
PH 716·759·1058 FAX 716·759·0731 EMAIL OFFICE@EAGLESWINGS.TO
WEBSITE : WWW.EAGLESWINGS.TO

FOR MORE INFORMATION CALL
1 800 51WINGS

MINISTERING GLOBALLY.

{THE JOURNAL}

Kairos
WHERE TIME AND DESTINY MEET

K | KAIROS PUBLISHING

Kairos is a timely **prophetic journal** and resource for the body of Christ. Centering on a key pertinent theme, each issue trumpets **a vital message** for the Body of Messiah. Regular columns include East Coast Update, Israel Update, International Update, as well as contributing authors such as Robert Stearns, Joseph Garlington, Sam Hinn, Frank Damazio, Larry Kreider, Dan Juster, JoAnn McFatter, and many more.

TO RECEIVE YOUR
COMPLIMENTARY ISSUE CALL
1 800 51WINGS

IT'S ABOUT TIME.